The Village Hall

A Comedy Play

Ashley Burgoyne

Copyright © Ashley Burgoyne 2018

ashleyburgoyne.wixsite.com/writerandcomposer

ashleyburgoynewriter@gmail.com

First Edition published in 2018

All rights whatsoever in this play are strictly reserved and applications for permission to perform it, etc., must be made in advance, before rehearsals begin, direct to the author at ashleyburgoynewriter@gmail.com

ISBN-13: 978-1981453092

ISBN-10: 1981453091

No one shall make any changes in this title for the purpose of production. No part of this book may be reproduced, stored in a retrieval system, or transmitted in any form, by any means, now known or yet to be invented, including mechanical, electronic, photocopying, recording, videotaping, or otherwise, without the prior written permission of the author. No one shall upload this title, or part of this title, to any social media websites.

THE VILLAGE HALL

First presented at The Atrium Theatre, North Walsham, Norfolk on 7th July 2017 by Stage Direct Amateur Drama Group, with the following cast of characters:

Derek	Derek Bull
Marjorie	Robin Spruce
Tyler	Robert Wright
Tia	Shania Waterson
Sarah	Serena Cain
Tom	David Starling
Laura	Melissa Collin
Giuseppe	Grant Barker
Daisy	Daisy Groom

Directed by Ashley Burgoyne

Characters

Derek, 50s, Chairman of the Parish Committee
Marjorie, 70s, his secretary on the Committee
Tyler, early 20s, member of the Committee
Tia, late teens, Tyler's girlfriend and member of the Committee
Sarah, late 30s, member of the Committee
Tom, 40s, Sarah's friend and member of the Committee
Laura, 40s, Tom's wife and leader of the amateur drama group
Giuseppe, late 20s, Tia's brother
Daisy, early 20s, Giuseppe's girlfriend

To be able to perform this play, the original score and CD containing the backing track for the original song 'Now or Never (If the Game is to be Won),' which is performed in Act 2, scenes 4 and 5, needs to be obtained, along with a performance licence from the author.

Please email: ashleyburgoynewriter@gmail.com

ACT I

Scene 1

Present Day. A Wednesday evening. 7:15pm.
A Parish Committee meeting.
A Village Hall. A row of tables along the centre of the hall with plastic chairs along one side and at each end. A pile of paper and pencils in the middle of the tables. Off stage, one side, is the entrance door. Off stage, the other side, is the door to the adjoining kitchen. There's a tall pot plant at each end of the hall.
Derek, an upright man aged in his 50s, enters from outside. He is holding a clipboard and wearing a black tracksuit with white stripes down the arms and legs. On the front, left breast of the tracksuit top are the words 'Village Games.' On the back it says 'Village Games, Upper Kingham, Team Manager.'
Derek starts to precisely place a piece of paper and a pencil in front of each chair. The pencil, which is sharpened at both ends, is placed above each piece of paper, where a dessert spoon might be placed if it was cutlery. He straightens up the occasional chair as well. His clipboard remains tucked under his arm throughout.
Marjorie enters, 70s. She holds a notepad and pen.

MARJORIE   Good evening, Derek.

DEREK   *(looking up)* Ah, Marjorie. Nice to see you. *(Carrying on with his pencil and paper straightening)* How are you?

Throughout the following Derek is clearly absorbed in his work and not listening

MARJORIE   Ok, I guess. Although I did have a fall last week. This new hip isn't as good as the other. Malcolm tried to lift me up, but that brought on his asthma. And Clara, you remember Clara?

DEREK   *(without lifting his head)* mmmm.

MARJORIE   She ran away again. Four days this time. I think someone else must be putting food out for her. I think it might be that new couple feeding her this time. The ones at 42. The Bakers.

DEREK	*(stopping and looking up)* The what?
MARJORIE	Bakers.
DEREK	Who are?
MARJORIE	My new neighbours. The ones at 42.
DEREK	Are they? That could be handy for the Village Games. Some fresh bread and cakes and stuff. *(Marjorie goes to correct Derek, but he's in a flow now!)* Anyway; glad to hear you're keeping well. *(Looking down at his clipboard)* Now, last month's minutes, Marjorie; two commas and a colon missing. But we've had worse, haven't we?
MARJORIE	*(submissively)* Yes, we have Derek. Sorry.
DEREK	At least it wasn't as bad as the hard copy you sent me four months ago when that cat of yours, erm, Katie…
MARJORIE	Clara.
DEREK	Yes, that's it, Clara, urinated all over it.
MARJORIE	Oh, it wasn't all over it, Derek, just the corner.
DEREK	But you still sent it to me.
MARJORIE	I had dried it on the radiator.
DEREK	I could tell. Not only did it smell, but the corner was crispy! When I ask for a hard copy, I don't literally mean hard!
MARJORIE	Sorry, Derek. I should have printed off another one for you.
DEREK	Yes, well, that's all water under the bridge, so to speak. Two commas and a colon; quite a success, then. *(Marjorie looks sheepish)* Right, tonight's the big one, Marjorie. Village Games planning! *(Derek taps the logo on his tracksuit)*

2

MARJORIE   I see you've changed the back of your tracksuit this year, Derek.

DEREK   Ah! You saw that did you?

MARJORIE   Yes, as I came in.

DEREK   *(turning around)* Do you like it?

MARJORIE   Erm, yes, Derek. Lovely. But we all know you're the manager, don't we?

DEREK   Yes, I know *you* all know I'm the manager, but not everyone knows!

MARJORIE   I'm sure they do, Derek, you have been running it for over 20 years.

DEREK   23, Marjorie, 23.

MARJORIE   Exactly. So, we all do know.

DEREK   Well, no harm in making sure certain people don't forget. Particularly those from Lower Kingham.

MARJORIE   Oh, I see. You mean Giuseppe?

DEREK   Yes.

MARJORIE   He didn't mean anything, when he said that.

~~**DEREK**   No.~~

~~**MARJORIE**   Just sporting banter.~~

~~**DEREK**   Quite.~~

MARJORIE   I'm sure he won't bring it up again.

DEREK   No.

Pause. Tyler enters, early 20s, clearly fit and sporty. He has his arm round Tia, late teens and only interested in Tyler

TYLER Evening all.

Marjorie smiles warmly at the young couple, Derek looks at Tyler with discomfort

MARJORIE Oh, hello Tyler, how are you?

TYLER Oh, I'm fine thank you Mrs Carter.

MARJORIE How about you, Tia?

TIA *(eyes firmly on Tyler)* mmmm?

MARJORIE Are you keeping well?

TIA *(struggling to glance across)* Oh, yes, thank you, Mrs Carter. Very well.

TYLER Hi, Derek. Want a hand with those pencils?

DEREK No thank you, Tyler. I can manage.

TYLER So, what's the main topic of discussion tonight then, Derek?

DEREK *(standing upright and trying not to get annoyed)* I think you already know, Tyler. I did email everyone an agenda.

TYLER *(clearly trying to wind Derek up)* Oh yes, the hedge round the bowling green and that barn conversion application. That was it.

DEREK *(tapping the logo on his chest)* The Village Games, Tyler, the Village Games!

TYLER Oh yes, the Village Games. *(Sitting)* I should have noticed your tracksuit top there.

TIA *(taking in the tracksuit top)* Oh yes, *(sitting)* my brother will be jealous of that tracksuit top.

DEREK   Yes, Tia, well, it was your brother who started with the wording on his sweater last year.

TIA   But his only said 'Coach.' Nothing else.

DEREK   Yes, well, needs must, Tia, needs must.

MARJORIE   And it was *you* who kept calling him 'bus,' Derek.

DEREK   Yes, thank you Marjorie. We all know that was down to Ms Bland's elderflower wine.

TYLER   Down to Ms Bland's fifth elderflower wine, more like!

DEREK   Thank you, Tyler. Just a few small beverages after losing the games for the first time in ten years. That was all.

MARJORIE   It was perfectly understandable, Derek.

TIA   Well, don't worry. Giuseppe hasn't got his name or coach or manager or anything like that on his top this year.

~~**DEREK**   Really?~~

~~**TIA**   Really.~~

~~**DEREK**   *(smiling smugly)* Nothing at all?~~

~~**TIA**   Nothing.~~

~~**DEREK**   Marvellous.~~

TIA   'Coz there's no room.

DEREK   *(bemused)* Excuse me?

TIA   There's no room.

DEREK   What do you mean 'no room?'

TIA   'Coz the advert's so big.

DEREK What advert?

TIA The one on his back. The sponsor he got.

Momentary silence as Derek starts to fume

DEREK The sponsor!? How on earth did he get a sponsor?

TIA 'Coz Lower Kingham won last year he went and got a sponsor.

DEREK But I've been trying for years to get a sponsor. Who sponsored him?

TIA The arcade on the prom.

DEREK You're joking! I've asked them several times.

TYLER Maybe they liked the fact that someone new had won the games.

DEREK Thank you, Tyler. That really helps.

TYLER Sorry, but....

MARJORIE *(interrupting)* I think you should keep quiet, Tyler.

TYLER Right.

DEREK What does this sponsor say, Tia?

TIA 'Spencer's Arcade supports Lower Kingham.'

DEREK Oh, they do, do they!

MARJORIE Well I never! How dare they. That's the last time I use one of their grab machines.

DEREK I can't believe... *(Taking in what Marjorie's just said)* You gamble, Marjorie?

MARJORIE I'd hardly call it gambling, Derek. Just the occasional grab in the arcade, that's all.

DEREK Grab in the arcade!? It's the thin end of the wedge, Marjorie. The thin end of the wedge.

MARJORIE Surely you approaching Spencer as a sponsor is the thin end of the wedge too?

DEREK Needs must, Marjorie, needs must. Anyway, someone's got to try and get your money back, haven't they? From all that unnecessary grabbing I mean. *(He demonstrates a grabbing claw)*

TYLER I bet you never won, did you Mrs Carter?

MARJORIE I did once. A little fluffy tiger.

~~**TIA** Aah.~~

MARJORIE Very sweet it was. I gave it to my granddaughter.

~~**TIA** Aah.~~

DEREK Can we get back to the point?

MARJORIE I can't remember what the point was.

TYLER Neither can I!

DEREK Sponsorship. Lower Kingham has some and we don't.

MARJORIE A bit late now, isn't it?

DEREK It's never too late, Marjorie. We'll add it to the agenda.

MARJORIE Really?

DEREK Really.

TYLER I wouldn't worry about it, Derek. As Tia says, you won't have room for 'Team Manager' and all those other words if you get sponsored.

DEREK I'll find room.

Tom enters, 40s. With him is Sarah, 30s

TOM (*mid sentence*) ... I couldn't believe they'd done it again.

SARAH It seems quite ridiculous, now.

MARJORIE Hello you two!

TOM Oh, hello Marjorie.

SARAH Hi everyone.

Tyler gives a cursory wave. Tia smiles

DEREK Sarah, Tom.

TOM Derek, how are you?

DEREK I'm very well, thank you Tom. Yourself?

TOM Fine, thanks. Apart from spending the weekend at the In-Laws, again.

DEREK Ah. They haven't had another have they?

TOM 'fraid so. That's what I was telling Sarah as we came in.

SARAH Quite ridiculous.

DEREK How many is it now?

TOM 17.

DEREK 17!

TOM Yes.

SARAH (*sitting*) See. Quite ridiculous.

TIA Excuse me, but what's quite ridiculous.

DEREK Ah, Tia, you don't know of Tom's In-Laws, do you?

TIA	Erm, no.
TYLER	Neither do I.
DEREK	Would you like to explain, Tom? Or shall I?
TOM	Be my guest, Derek.
DEREK	*(taking a deep breath)* Tom's parents-in-law have a smallholding up North, don't they, Tom.
TOM	Yes, edge of the moors.
DEREK	They keep a few animals; horses mostly isn't it?
TOM	Yes.
DEREK	But a few others. Dogs, chickens and so on. But it's when they die isn't it, Tom.
TOM	Yes.
TYLER	Why? What happens then?
DEREK	They have them cremated.
TIA	Sounds fair enough.
TYLER	And then they scatter the ashes on their land?
TOM	If only they would.
DEREK	No. They get the ashes back in a wooden casket. To keep.
TYLER	Ok. So what's the problem?
DEREK	17, Tyler. That's the problem. 17!
TYLER	Ah.
TOM	And they're all in the spare bedroom. The one where me and Laura sleep!

TYLER	Ah.
TIA	That can't be too bad. 17 little wooden boxes. Must be quite pretty!
TOM	Little! Have you ever seen a wooden casket for a horse?
TIA	Erm, no. Only one for a rabbit we once had.
TOM	Well, let me tell you. The latest horse box acts as a unit for the TV at the end of the bed.
TIA	Oh, I see.
TYLER	And the other 16?
TOM	All over the shop!
TYLER	Really?
TOM	Oh, yes. Two Shetland ponies; two bedside tables. Dogs and cats all over the chest of drawers and so on.
TYLER	Ah.
TOM	God knows where they're gonna put Brutus when he goes.
TIA	Who's Brutus?
TOM	The Shire horse.
TYLER	Ah.
TOM	We live in fear of when we turn up and the Shire horse has gone!
TYLER	I can imagine.
TOM	Then there's the equipment.
TIA	Equipment?

TOM Oh, yes. Each casket has a picture of the animal by it, or on top of it. Then there's their collar or lead placed with it.

TYLER Don't tell me the horses' saddles are there as well?

Everyone laughs

TOM You may well laugh, but they were. We managed to get them to down-size just to harnesses and things.

TIA And these are by the caskets?

TOM Yep!

TIA Even the ones that are bedside tables?

TOM Yep. Many a time I've gone for a glass of water in the night and picked up a horses' bit or something similar!

Everyone laughs again

MARJORIE Poor you. Come and sit down and I'll put the urn on for a nice cuppa.

Everyone starts to sit as Marjorie goes out to the kitchen

TOM Thanks, Marjorie.

DEREK *(taking his seat at the head of the table)* That sounds just the ticket, Marjorie. We'd better get a move on as that new am dram group are coming in at 9pm to audition for their first play.

Marjorie returns with a plate of biscuits

TIA *(excitedly)* We know. We're reading for a part, aren't we Tyler?

TYLER *(almost as excited)* Yes, we are!

MARJORIE Krap.

11

Everyone looks at Marjorie, stunned

DEREK   I beg your pardon, Marjorie!?

MARJORIE   Krap. That's what they're calling themselves. Kingham Regional Amateur Players. K. R. A. P. Krap.

Tia giggles

DEREK   Surely not!

TOM   No they're not, Marjorie. They're going to be called Kingham Amateur Dramatic Society.

TYLER   KADS.

DEREK   Yes, well, that's not that much better. How do you know what they're going to be called, Tom?

TOM   'Coz it's Laura's thing.

DEREK   Laura's going to be running this group?

TOM   Yep. It's something she's wanted to do for a while.

DEREK   Well, good luck to her!

SARAH   Do you not think she's up to it, Derek? I mean, she is Head of Drama at the High School.

DEREK   Oh, no. It's not that. I know she'd be ok with the drama and all that. It's just the organisational side of it. *(Picking up his clipboard)* Does she have a clipboard?

MARJORIE   Oh, Derek.

DEREK   What?

MARJORIE   Never mind. Shall we make a start?

DEREK   Yes. Before those KADS arrive!

Lights fade to blackout

Scene 2

Lights up on:
The same. 8:55pm. Laura enters, 40s, slightly dizzy 'bohemian' looking.
She carries a bag and a CD/cassette player.

TOM	*(getting up)* Hello, darling. *(He kisses her on her cheek)*
DEREK	*(looking up from his clipboard)* Ah! Here she is! Our very own David Lean!
SARAH	Hardly, Derek!
DEREK	I beg your pardon?
SARAH	Laura is a woman.
DEREK	Yes. I'm fully aware of that, Sarah.
SARAH	Impress her by naming her after a female director.
DEREK	Oh, right, I see. Sorry, Laura.
LAURA	That's ok, Derek. I'm happy with David Lean!
DEREK	No, no. Sarah's right. Erm. *(Pause)* Here she is! Our very own. *(Further pause)* No, I'm sorry. I just can't think of one.
TYLER	Kathryn Bigelow.
DEREK	Who?
TYLER	Kathryn Bigelow.
TIA	Oh, yes. She won an Oscar a few years ago for The Hurt Locker, didn't she?
TYLER	That's the one.
DEREK	I've no idea who you're talking about.
TYLER	Oh, Derek!

13

LAURA It really doesn't matter. I'd just like to get started.

DEREK Yes, righto Laura. Off you go everyone. Let's leave Laura to set up. She's bound to have all her budding actors turning up in a minute.

Derek is the only one to get up

TYLER We're staying.

DEREK Yes, I know you and Tia are.

TYLER No, we're all staying.

Derek looks around

DEREK All of you?

TYLER Yes.

~~**TIA** Uh, huh.~~

~~**SARAH** Yes.~~

DEREK Even you, Marjorie?

MARJORIE Yes.

~~**DEREK** Oh.~~

LAURA Is there any reason why Marjorie can't join us, Derek?

DEREK Oh, no. No reason at all, Laura. I just didn't think it would be her sort of thing. That's all.

TOM None of us are sure if it's any of our sort of thing, Derek.

LAURA That's why we're holding this read-through. Want to give it a try, Derek?

DEREK What, me?

14

LAURA	Yes, why not?
DEREK	Oh, I don't think it's my sort of thing really.
TIA	Go on, Derek. I'm sure you'd be good.
DEREK	Well, that's very kind of you to say so, Tia. But, I've got the Village Games five-a-side tournament to plan and then I must get on the oche.
TIA	The what?
DEREK	The oche. Darts. I must practise some darts. For the Village Games.
TIA	Tyler's good at darts, aren't you, Tyler?

Tyler goes to answer, but Derek interjects

DEREK	I know Tyler's good at darts. He kept telling me last year he was good at darts.
MARJORIE	But you didn't listen, did you, Derek? You still insisted on playing Giuseppe yourself, didn't you?
DEREK	Yes, well, I'd never lost a Village Games darts match had I. No reason to not play him was there?
MARJORIE	Apart from the fact Tia told you he'd played for the county.
DEREK	Thank you Marjorie. I think that's quite enough. That's why I'm putting more practice in this year, isn't it!

Pause

TIA	You beat him the other day, didn't you, Tyler?
TYLER	Yeah.
DEREK	Why were you playing Giuseppe at darts?
TIA	You often practise with him, don't you?

15

TYLER Yeah.

DEREK You practise with the enemy? *(Tia glares at Derek)* Sorry, I mean with Giuseppe?

TIA He's not the enemy, Derek, he's my brother.

DEREK I know, I'm sorry Tia, no offence meant.

TIA Tyler practises with him because, after you lost to Giuseppe last year, he thought you might ask him to play the darts match in this year's Games!

DEREK *(looking at Tyler)* Ah, well, no. One defeat in 23 Village Games is not enough to stop old Deadly Darts Derek from playing. *(Picking up his clipboard and heading for the door)* Sorry.

TYLER That's ok, Derek. I don't mind. Just give me a shout if you need any pointers!

Derek gives Tyler a glare as he leaves the Village Hall

MARJORIE You two really mustn't tease him.

TIA We don't mean to. We just want the village to win the Games back this year, and we won't with him playing the darts.

TYLER Silly old ….

LAURA *(interjecting)* Thank you, Tyler. It's my time now. Drama time! *(She presses 'play' on the CD player. We hear 'There's No Business, Like Show Business.' Everyone exchanges pained glances. Tom puts his head in his hands as Sarah stifles a giggle)* *(Stopping the music)* Good! Now we're out of Parish Committee and Village Games nonsense; we can begin!

TOM *(lifting his head out of his hands)* Great.

LAURA And breathe!

TOM What?

LAURA Breathe, everyone. *(Demonstrating)* In through the nose and out through the mouth.

Everyone looks at Tom for assistance

TOM *(sotto)* I thought I suggested you didn't do the breathing thing, Laura.

Marjorie has subconsciously started the breathing exercise

LAURA I know you did, Tom, but I've decided it's probably more necessary than I first thought; seeing as this read-through is on the back of a nasty old Committee meeting!

TOM *(sotto)* We're not pupils at your school, Laura. We're adults!

LAURA *(ignoring him)* That's it Marjorie. Everyone follow Marjorie. *(Exaggerating a demonstration)* In through the nose and out through the mouth.

Everyone slowly joins in, very reluctantly. As some sort of rhythmic breathing starts to build, Giuseppe enters. He's late 20s, smartly dressed with a rough edge. Just behind him is his girlfriend, Daisy. She's early 20s and over dressed and over made-up for the proceedings. They both stand and stare with amusement

TOM *(seeing an opportunity to stop 'breathing' jumps up to greet them. Shaking hands)* Ah, Giuseppe, Daisy, great to see you both.

GIUSEPPE Hi, Tom. Hi everyone.

TIA Hi, Zep.

GIUSEPPE Didn't interrupt anything, did we?

LAURA *(straightening herself up as she sees Giuseppe)* No, no. Just some warm-up exercises; that's all.

GIUSEPPE   Oh, I see.

LAURA   Just some deep breathing; like this. *(She holds her stomach in and sticks her chest out to exaggerate her breathing – and everything else!)*

TOM   *(under Laura's exaggerated breathing)* Don't encourage her, Giuseppe, please!

DAISY   Tom's right, Giuseppe, don't tease her. You know she's got a thing for you!

GIUSEPPE   You're right. Sorry, Tom.

TOM   It doesn't bother me really. Just a bit embarrassing. *(Pause)* Which is nothing new, really!

~~LAURA   *(finishing her final breath)* Like that, you see?~~

~~GIUSEPPE   *(sitting)* Yeah, great.~~

~~DAISY   *(sitting)* Shame we missed it.~~

GIUSEPPE   Yeah. Sorry we're a bit late. ~~We were~~ [I was] waiting in the car until Derek had gone.

SARAH   Why's that?

GIUSEPPE   Oh, you know what Derek's like, Sarah. I don't want to get him too flustered this far ahead of the Village Games. I can do without another lecture on staying in my own Village Hall.

SARAH   Did he really say that?

GIUSEPPE   Yeah, a few months ago when I was picking Tia up from her Pilates class.

~~SARAH   Oh, dear. I never knew that.~~

~~GIUSEPPE   Silly old~~…

18

LAURA	*(interjecting)* Thank you, Giuseppe. Can we now get on with some drama? *(She leans towards the CD player as if to turn 'There's No Business, Like Show Business' on once more)*
TOM	*(putting his hand in the way of Laura's)* Can we leave the music now, Laura, love?
LAURA	*(slightly put out)* Oh, ok. *(Addressing everyone)* Welcome everyone to the first ever meeting of the Kingham Amateur Dramatic Society. Now, to make all of this official we're going to need to form a KADS Committee with Chairperson, Treasurer, Secretary, Members and all that. But I thought I'd address that in the next few days so that we can just do the fun stuff tonight by trying a read-through.
TIA	Great! What play are we going to do?
LAURA	*(handing out scripts)* Well; I'll pass these around. There should be enough for one each.
MARJORIE	What's it called? My copy doesn't seem to have a title!
LAURA	Ah, well, none of them have a title on, Marjorie, as it's my own work and I've yet to decide on a title.
~~**MARJORIE**~~	~~Oh, ok~~.
LAURA	Now then, it's basically a love story, with lots of crossed wires and things. What I think I should do is give you each a part to read and just go for it and hopefully the story will explain itself as we go along. If it doesn't I'll have to rewrite it!
TOM	*(putting his hand on Laura's)* It'll be fine, love. It's really good. It made perfect sense when you let me read it through the other day.
LAURA	Thank you, darling. *(Turning to the others)* Now then, the male lead; Carl, I'd like to be read first by you, Giuseppe.

TOM	Oh.
LAURA	Alright, darling?
TOM	Fine, yes, it's just that I thought you were going to let me read for that part.
GIUSEPPE	I don't mind letting Tom read for that part, Laura.
LAURA	It's just a read-through, Tom. I'll give you a chance, darling and….

Pause

TOM	And what?
LAURA	And…. You're a bit too old for Carl really, darling.
TOM	Oh.
LAURA	Sorry, darling. I thought you might have worked that out for yourself when you read it the other day.
TOM	Well, I don't think I look my age, do I?

Pause

	(As no one responds) Oh.
MARJORIE	Of course you don't, Tom.
SARAH	*(smiling)* Definitely not!
TOM	*(smiling back sheepishly)* Thank you. *(Recovering slightly)* Anyway; I thought the quality of my singing voice might sway it my way.
GIUSEPPE	Singing?
TOM	Yes, singing.
GIUSEPPE	I didn't know there was any singing in it!

LAURA	Oh, yes, it's a musical. Well, not really a musical, but it does have a few self-penned songs in it. Just to add to it. Didn't I say that?
GIUSEPPE	No.
LAURA	Is that a problem?
TIA	*(giggling)* Giuseppe singing? Oh dear.
GIUSEPPE	Alright, sis. I'm not that bad.
TIA	Not that bad! You're terrible!
GIUSEPPE	Oh, come on now.
~~**TIA**~~	~~Help me out here, Daisy. You must have heard him~~ sing?
~~**DAISY**~~	~~Well I've heard him make noises in the shower. I suppose you could call it singing. I suppose.~~
~~**GIUSEPPE**~~	~~Charming!~~
~~**DAISY**~~	~~Sorry, love. Just being honest~~.
LAURA	Do you want to try, Giuseppe? I'll let you know if you can sing or not.
GIUSEPPE	Erm, maybe you should let someone else try first.
LAURA	*(leaning across to hold Giuseppe's hand)* I'm sure you'll sound lovely. Let me listen to you.

Everyone looks awkward at Laura's obvious flirting. Tom shakes his head as Giuseppe shrugs in his direction

GIUSEPPE	*(trying to extricate his hand)* No, I really think I'll let someone else have a go. I feel like I've lost my confidence now.
TOM	*(removing Laura's hand from Giuseppe's)* Come on love. It's up to Giuseppe, isn't it?

21

LAURA	*(weakly smiling at Giuseppe)* Of course, of course. *(Pause)* Right then. Tyler; can you read the part of Carl, please?
TYLER	Erm, certainly.
TOM	*(incredulously)* What?
LAURA	You're still too old, darling.
TOM	*(sitting back in his chair and folding his arms)* Huh!
LAURA	~~And you can read Bella, the female lead if you don't mind please, Daisy.~~
DAISY	~~Ok.~~
TIA	What about me. Can't I have a try at that part?
GIUSEPPE	Maybe Laura's heard that the bad singing runs in the family!?
TIA	Oi!
LAURA	Of course you can, Tia. ~~But one at a time and Daisy first, ok?~~
TIA	~~*(a little reluctantly)* Ok.~~
LAURA	Then we have Bella's father. You can read that part, Tom.
TOM	Father!?
LAURA	Yes, Tom, father.
TOM	This is getting worse by the minute.
LAURA	You are, what, more than 20 years older than Daisy. Plenty old enough to be her father.
TOM	Yes, well, true…. But I don't look it!

SARAH	Of course you don't, Tom.
TOM	Thank you. Again. Sarah. *(They exchange smiles)*
LAURA	And Bella's mother can be read by you, Sarah.
SARAH	Ok.
TOM	Oh, come on, Laura, love. Sarah? ~~Daisy's mother?~~
LAURA	I think you'll find she's just about old enough, aren't you Sarah?
SARAH	*(humouring Laura)* Yes, I think you'll find I am.
TOM	Maybe so; but she certainly doesn't look it.
LAURA	Make-up.
TOM	Pardon?
LAURA	If people think that Sarah doesn't look old enough we'll use make-up.
TOM	If make-up's getting involved, why can't I have some to make me look a bit younger so I can play the lead?
LAURA	Because we're a new Company, Tom, and we don't have that much make-up!

Smiles around as Tom leans back in his chair and folds his arms in disgust

	Now, who else do we need. Erm, Marjorie. Now then Marjorie; Carl has been brought up by his grandmother, so I'd like you to read that part.
MARJORIE	Ok, sounds lovely.
GIUSEPPE	And you better be good at it, Marjorie, 'coz unless Derek comes back we've got no other old women who can play that part!

MARJORIE What was that, dear?

Daisy and Tia giggle

SARAH Come on, Giuseppe, I don't think that's quite appropriate.

GIUSEPPE Sorry, just a joke. Sorry.

LAURA Yes, well, we've just got you and Tia to cast for the first read-through now, haven't we. I tell you what; you try any other male part you come across, Giuseppe and you try any other female part that you see, Tia. None of the other parts are quite as big so try them all and we'll see which ones fit. Ok?

~~**TIA** Sure.~~

~~**GIUSEPPE** Fine.~~

MARJORIE Who *is* going to play all the other parts, Laura?

LAURA Oh, don't worry, there's plenty of staff at the school who have said they don't mind taking on small parts. We'll save the smallest for them.

~~**MARJORIE** Ok.~~

LAURA Now then. Let me set the scene.

GIUSEPPE Before you do, Laura, can I just ask a quick question?

LAURA *(not wanting to miss an opportunity, she quickly leans across and takes hold of Giuseppe's hand once more)* Anything, Giuseppe, dear.

Tom shakes his head

GIUSEPPE *(allowing Laura to hold his hand this time)* Where are we going to perform this play?

LAURA Oh, I don't know, Giuseppe. It's early days. The school hall, maybe. Or maybe in here? *(She indicates the Villlage Hall with her free hand)*

GIUSEPPE Here? You don't want to put it on in here! Why don't you try and put it on at the theatre?

Tom removes Laura's hand from Giuseppe's

LAURA The theatre? Oh, I don't think so, Giuseppe. It'll be my first production. I don't think I should be aiming that high.

GIUSEPPE I think you should.

LAURA Do you?

GIUSEPPE *(smiling)* Yes.

LAURA *(looking a little embarrassed)* Oh!

TYLER And I agree.

LAURA Do you, Tyler?

TYLER Yes. Just because it's your first production, doesn't mean that you can't aim high.

GIUSEPPE That's right, Tyler. Aim for the top, Laura. *(He smiles at Laura, who visibly melts. Tom shakes his head again)*

TIA Have you two been drinking?!

GIUSEPPE No, sis, I just think we can perform somewhere better than here. *(He looks around the hall)*

LAURA Well, that's very kind of you both to say so, thank you.

GIUSEPPE So, that's a yes to the theatre, then, Laura?

LAURA *(melting again)* It's an 'I'll look into it!' ok?

GIUSEPPE Ok.

Laura continues to gaze into Giuseppe's eyes as he sits back in his seat

TOM Shall we get on, Laura?

LAURA *(still staring at Giuseppe)* Mmm?

TOM The scene, love. You were about to set the scene.

LAURA What? *(Snapping out of it)* Oh, yes, the scene. Yes. Let me set the scene.

During the following the lights fade to blackout

We open with Bella's bedroom. She's sitting at her desk, staring out of her window. Books and papers are strewn across her desk. She's a university student and she's at home on study leave, but all she can think of is Gius... Carl....

Scene 3

Lights up on:
The same, 10:10pm.

LAURA I think we should call it a night, there. Don't you?

MARJORIE I think so, Laura. My Horlicks is calling me!

DAISY Do we have to leave it there? It's just getting exciting and I really want to know what Bella says as a reply to that Tweet!

LAURA Ah, well, that comes out in the next number, Daisy.

TOM Yes, Daisy, the next number's a real tweet.

No response, except for a smile from Sarah

LAURA Thank you darling.

TOM Yes, well, just trying to inject a little humour into the proceedings, that's all.

LAURA Mmmm. Right; same time next week and I'll tell you who's got what part. Ok?

Talking over each other as they get up to leave

GIUSEPPE Great.

~~**DAISY** Lovely.~~

~~**TIA** See you all next week, then.~~

~~**TYLER** Bye.~~

Laura and Tom busy themselves collecting in the play scripts

MARJORIE I'll just go and tidy up in the kitchen.

SARAH Oh, it's alright Marjorie. I'll do it.

MARJORIE   Are you sure, dear.

SARAH   Oh, yes. You've got a Horlicks and a Malcolm calling you….

MARJORIE   And a Clara.

SARAH   Oh, yes. And a Clara. I've got nothing calling me, so you go on home and leave it all to me.

MARJORIE   Oh, thank you, Sarah. You are a dear.

SARAH   You're welcome, Marjorie. Look after that hip, now, won't you?

MARJORIE   I'll do my best. Night all.

SARAH   'Night, Marjorie.

TOM   ~~Oh, yes, goodnight, Marjorie. Take care~~.

LAURA   ~~Bye. See you next week~~.

MARJORIE   ~~Oh, yes, definitely. That was great fun!~~ *(She exits)*

SARAH   Ah, bless her. I'll be in the kitchen clearing up. *(She exits to the kitchen)*

LAURA   Do you think it went alright, darling?

TOM   Yes, fine. Well, not bad for a first read-through.

LAURA   Once you'd had your tizzy.

TOM   What tizzy?

LAURA   All that 'I don't look my age' nonsense.

TOM   Yes, well, maybe it was all nonsense, but you could have let me read the lead part first. Even if you were going to give it to Giuseppe or Tyler. And maybe not shown me up in front of everyone.

LAURA	I'm sorry, darling. I didn't mean to do that.
TOM	Well, you did. A little bit of support, now and again, wouldn't go amiss.
LAURA	I said I'm sorry, darling.
TOM	I am a policeman. Just because I'm out of uniform doesn't mean you can belittle me.
LAURA	*(getting annoyed)* I did say I'm sorry, darling. Now, can we go?
TOM	You go. I'll wait for Sarah, lock up and post the key back through Derek's on my way home.
LAURA	Ok. Just don't be long. You know Derek likes the key to be returned by half ten.
TOM	I know. See you soon.
LAURA	Bye. *(She picks up all her stuff and exits)*

Sarah returns from the kitchen

SARAH	*(smiling)* Safe to come in?
TOM	*(returning the smile)* Heard all that, did you?
SARAH	You know that kitchen, Tom. You can hear everything from in there.
TOM	I know.
SARAH	*(moving closer)* Why do you let her get away with things?
TOM	I love her.
SARAH	Do you?
TOM	Yes.

SARAH Real love?

TOM *(shrugging)* I don't know what that is.

SARAH *(moving even closer)* It's the love you're supposed to act on. That's what real love is.

TOM Then it must be real love because I acted on it. I married her.

SARAH But, is it still real love?

TOM I think you should go home, Sarah.

SARAH Don't shut me out, Tom.

TOM I'm not shutting you out; you're just asking me a question I don't know the answer to. Love changes. We change. Love changes with it.

SARAH It doesn't have to.

TOM It does, Sarah. You haven't got a partner or children. You're still on the bottom rung of the love ladder.

~~**SARAH** Charming!~~

~~**TOM** What?~~

SARAH Bottom rung of the love ladder! You make me sound like a child.

~~**TOM** I'm sorry. That's not what I meant.~~

SARAH I have had sex before, you know!

~~**TOM** *(embarrassed by the direction this conversation is taking)* Yes, I'm sure you have.~~

SARAH Lots of times.

~~**TOM** Yes.~~

SARAH ~~That's not to say I sleep around.~~

TOM ~~No, no.~~

SARAH ~~That's not what I meant.~~

TOM ~~No.~~

SARAH ~~Not at all.~~

TOM No. *(Pause)* I didn't mean you're inexperienced. Just that love changes when you spend all your time with the same person. It's not a bad thing. It just happens. *(Taking Sarah's hand)* ~~Do you know what I mean, sweet Sarah?~~

SARAH ~~*(smiling)* You've always called me sweet Sarah, haven't you?~~

TOM ~~Well I've known you a long time and you're.... sweet!~~

SARAH ~~Have you ever wanted to call me anything else?~~

TOM ~~Like what?~~

SARAH ~~Like 'saucy Sarah' or 'sexy Sarah?'~~

TOM Sarah. *(Removing his hand)* We've discussed this before. I'm married, I have two children and I'm a police officer.

SARAH *(raising her voice)* But she's mad! All those breathing exercises and showing you up.

TOM It's just the way she is.

SARAH With mad parents who make you sleep in the spare room with the dead animals.

TOM Not quite.

31

SARAH	It is, quite. Why don't you just stop defending her and doing what she wants all the time. Why don't you do what *you* want?
TOM	How do you know that this isn't what I want?
SARAH	*(moving closer)* Because I can see. In your eyes. Behind your eyes. You're looking for a way out. And that way out is me.
TOM	Sarah. *I* don't exist anymore. '*Me*' becomes '*we*' when you get married. My family is me.
SARAH	I....... just....... *(Screaming)* Aaagh!! *(She grabs Tom)* Can't you see I love you!
TOM	*(gently pulling her away)* But is it real love?
Pause	
SARAH	*(thumping Tom on the chest)* You're incorrigible. Do you know that?
TOM	I know. Come on let's go. Derek will be expecting his key back by now.
SARAH	I haven't finished in there yet. *(Indicating the kitchen)* Give me the key, I'll drop it off when I'm done. Should only take five minutes or so.
TOM	*(he passes the key to her)* Ok. But lock the door whilst you're in here on your own.
SARAH	Oh, really, Tom?
TOM	Yes, really, Sarah! I'm the policeman. I know what's best.
SARAH	Best for everyone else except yourself!
TOM	Maybe. But, besides that, it's in the insurance for this place and you don't want Derek getting upset, do you?

SARAH No, I don't. Off you go. I'll lock up behind you.

TOM Ok. Take care. I'll see you soon. *(He kisses her on the cheek. Sarah's kiss lingers a little longer)*

~~**SARAH** See you soon.~~

~~**TOM** Bye.~~

~~**SARAH** Bye.~~

Tom exits the Village Hall. Sarah follows him off stage, locks the door and returns

SARAH *(muttering to herself as she crosses the stage and exits to the kitchen)* Don't want to upset Derek, do we!

Silence for a short while

GIUSEPPE *(off stage)* Give it here. I'll do it.

TYLER *(off stage)* It's alright. It's turning.

GIUSEPPE *(off stage)* Are you sure? You're making hard work of it.

TYLER *(off stage)* Got it.

Tyler enters holding a key up. Giuseppe follows. Giuseppe's tone is more menacing, demonstrating that the Giuseppe everyone else sees is just a front for the real Giuseppe

TYLER It's bent, look.

GIUSEPPE Give it here. *(He takes the key from Tyler. Looking at it)* What do you expect. It's a dodgy copy. Got us in though, didn't it?

TYLER Where d'ya get it from again?

GIUSEPPE *(tapping the side of his nose)* Spencer; with an 'ask no questions' look.

TYLER	You sure there's no one here. The lights have been left on.
GIUSEPPE	Yeah, well, they do that these days, don't they. Leave lights on in places overnight so anyone nicking stuff can be seen.
TYLER	So we'll be seen then.
GIUSEPPE	Yes, but a) we're allowed in here, b) there's nothing to nick and c) no one comes up the lane at this time of night. We watched PC Tom lock up and go, didn't we? Don't worry, we'll be fine in here.
TYLER	But why are we in here?
GIUSEPPE	I've told you before. So there's no trace back to either mine or yours. Also; this place has a big table to spread the plans out on. Move yourself.

Giuseppe pushes Tyler to one side as he sits down at the table and produces some large scrolls of paper. He lays these on the table and puts weights on each corner such as car keys etc. Tyler sits next to Giuseppe and they both peer at the 'plans' in front of them

GIUSEPPE	Good, aren't they?
TYLER	*(peering closer)* Brilliant. Where did you get them from?
GIUSEPPE	~~Spencer.~~
TYLER	~~*(tapping the side of his nose)* With an 'ask no~~ questions' look?!
GIUSEPPE	~~*(winking)* That's the one~~.
TYLER	So; what's the plan?
GIUSEPPE	Well; early days yet, but, *(pointing at one plan)* this is the plan of the theatre and *(pointing at another)* this is the Building Society next door.

TYLER   Ok.

GIUSEPPE   And this is the adjoining wall.

TYLER   *(peering at the plans)* Even though we mentioned the theatre; how do we know that Laura's gonna put this musical play thing on there?

GIUSEPPE   We don't, but that's why we're in it. To persuade her.

TYLER   And if anyone can, you can!

GIUSEPPE   Yeah. You saw the way she looked at me tonight. She's putty in my hands, Tyler, putty in my hands.

TYLER   Yeah. Then on the last night of the show we break through the adjoining wall?

GIUSEPPE   Last night! I wanna be done by dress rehearsal at the latest.

TYLER   Why?

GIUSEPPE   'Coz I don't wanna get up on that stage. That's why!

TYLER   But the play's good.

GIUSEPPE   Tyler. Remember we're only doing the play to get access to the under-stage area so we can get to the wall adjoining the Building Society vault. Alright?

TYLER   So we nick the stuff and then not put on the show?

GIUSEPPE   Exactly.

TYLER   Talk about framing ourselves.

GIUSEPPE   What do you mean?

TYLER   We nick the stuff, disappear and not turn up for the show? Bit obvious really. Even for PC Tom!

GIUSEPPE Ah, yes, but Spencer reckons they'll cancel the show. Due to the break in.

TYLER They might. They might not. They might just cordon off the under-stage area. We don't know.

GIUSEPPE What do you suggest then?

TYLER Do the show. Better alibi. Putting all this effort in to the show gives us a better alibi.

GIUSEPPE Gives you a better chance to ponce around on stage you mean.

TYLER Not my fault that I can sing.

GIUSEPPE Huh. I can sing and I can call time too. *(Moving towards Tyler)* Call time on you and Tia. Just remember that when you're hitting the high notes.

TYLER *(attempting to stand up to Giuseppe)* I don't think Tia will stop seeing me just on your word.

GIUSEPPE No. You're probably right. She's soppy about you. I don't know why. But; if my word isn't strong enough to work, there's always Magaluf….

TYLER *(visibly gulping whilst stepping back from Giuseppe)* Now come on, Giuseppe.

GIUSEPPE *(slowly advancing on Tyler)* What?

TYLER What happens in Magaluf, stays in Magaluf, eh?

GIUSEPPE Unless it affects my little sister.

TYLER Oh, come on, Giuseppe. I told you, my drink was spiked.

GIUSEPPE And I told you it wasn't. *(Taking hold of Tyler's scruff/collar)* And who will Tia believe when it comes to an act of infidelity.

TYLER Oh, come on.

GIUSEPPE I think we both know the answer to that one, don't we?

TYLER Alright, alright. No need for that. *(Giuseppe lets go)* I said I'd help. I'm helping.

GIUSEPPE Then *you* can do what you want with your share and I can get out of this hole.

TYLER Ok.

GIUSEPPE Now, then. *(Looking back at the plans)* It's a four-man job. The person in the Building Society. Me, you and Spencer.

TYLER Who is the person in the Building Society?

GIUSEPPE You don't need to know.

TYLER Alright. What about Spencer?

GIUSEPPE What do you mean?

TYLER I mean, what actual part is he playing in all this?

GIUSEPPE This key *(holding up the Village Hall key),* these plans. All Spencer.

TYLER But what about the job itself? Person inside Building Society doing their bit. Me and you under the stage in the theatre doing our bit. Where's Spencer?

GIUSEPPE With us.

TYLER With us?

GIUSEPPE When the time comes, Spencer's gonna put himself forward to be in charge of props for the play. He'll be under the stage with us. Well, with me. You getting the main part is gonna put you on stage more than under it.

TYLER Well, the lead role is young. It had to be you or me.

GIUSEPPE   It would have been better if she'd given it to Tom. Would have kept him on stage more.

TYLER   I think his part's big enough to keep him on stage rather than under it.

GIUSEPPE   Hopefully. *(Clearing up the plans)* Let's put this all away. I'll catch up with Spencer soon and let you know the next step.

TYLER   Ok.

GIUSEPPE   Come on.

They exit

GIUSEPPE   *(off stage)* Bloody key!

Pause. Sarah enters from the kitchen

SARAH   *(talking to herself)* You know that kitchen, Tom. You can hear everything from in there!

She gives a wry smile as she exits the Village Hall. Lights fade to blackout

ACT II

Scene 1

Lights up on:
The same. A few days later. 6:45pm.
Sarah's sitting at the table. There's a pile of paper and pencils on the table. She appears pensive. Looking around her. Checking no one is around. Regularly checking towards the door. A moment. Tom comes in.

TOM Hi.

SARAH *(leaping up and wrapping her arms round Tom)* Oh, Tom. What are we going to do? What are we going to do?

TOM *(unwrapping Sarah's arms from around him)* It's alright love, it's alright.

SARAH How can it be? Giuseppe and Tyler are planning to break into the Building Society and we're all going to be accessories, or whatever you call it, to a crime!

TOM No we're not. Now then calm down. I've never seen you like this. You're normally the calmest person I know. I come to you when I need calm. You know that, don't you?

SARAH I know. Sorry. *(Calming a little)* Sorry.

TOM Right then. First things first. What excuse did you give Derek for wanting the key early?

SARAH I told him that I needed to sort some stuff out in the kitchen to make it easier for Marjorie. You know, with her hip.

TOM And did he buy that?

SARAH I think so. You know Derek. He doesn't go near the kitchen unless he has to, so he's got no idea what state it's in.

TOM	And have you mentioned what you overheard to anyone?
SARAH	No one. Just you. Why?
TOM	'Coz that's the way we've got to keep it, ok?
SARAH	Ok, but why?
TOM	I took your emails to my DCI. He asked if I believed what you said you'd heard, and if I trusted you.
SARAH	And what did you say?
TOM	I said yes, of course!
SARAH	*(smiling)* Good. Correct answer!
TOM	And he said that we now need evidence.
SARAH	Evidence?
TOM	Evidence. What you overheard isn't enough.
SARAH	Ok, so what do we do?
TOM	You do nothing. I, and the police, do something.
SARAH	Ok, what are you, and *the police,* going to do.
TOM	Well the thing is Giuseppe and Tyler are just one part of this *and* I got the impression from your email that Tyler was only helping so he could stay with Tia. Does that sound correct?
SARAH	He certainly seemed to be under some sort of threat from Giuseppe.
TOM	Ok, so Giuseppe and Tyler are my part of the problem. Other officers are on to Spencer – we've been watching him for years. That arcade is a front for a lot of dodgy dealings, I can tell you. And more officers are going to

	be trying to find out who the inside man is. The one at the Building Society.
SARAH	Ok. How are you going to get some evidence on Giuseppe and Tyler?
TOM	I'm going to bug this place!
SARAH	Bug it?
TOM	Yep. Tiny cameras and microphones everywhere.
SARAH	Where?
TOM	Ah, *(he taps the side of his nose)* now that would be telling! But we'll certainly cover the door so we can see them using the copied key you mentioned and then just the rest of the hall really. But I'm not going to tell you where. I don't want you smiling for the camera, do I?!
SARAH	And you want me to do nothing?
TOM	Exactly. Just be normal.
SARAH	You mean put lots of effort in to this play? A play that may never be performed?
TOM	*(shrugging)* That's just the way it is! *(Looking at his watch)* You better get in that kitchen 'coz Derek will be here soon. I'll put his blessed pencils and paper out.
SARAH	Ok. *(Going to leave, then turning)* This'll all be alright, won't it?
TOM	*(moving towards her)* It'll be fine. *(Taking her hands)* Trust me.
SARAH	*(smiling)* I do. *(She exits to the kitchen)*

Tom starts to lay the paper out, one sheet in front of each chair. He then places a pencil to the right-hand side of each piece of paper whilst humming the theme tune to a police television show such as Z-Cars!

Derek enters

DEREK   Evening, Tom.

TOM   *(looking up)* Oh, hello, Derek. How are you?

DEREK   Very well, thank you. You?

TOM   Oh, I'm fine.

DEREK   I wasn't expecting you to be up here so early.

TOM   Oh, I've only just arrived.

DEREK   And Sarah?

TOM   Oh, she's in the kitchen. Sorting stuff out.

DEREK   Good. *(Looking down at the paper and pencils)* Would you like me to take over from you?

TOM   *(placing the last pencil)* I think I'm done, Derek.

DEREK   Ah, well, I hope you don't mind but I'm just going to re-place the pencils.

TOM   Replace the pencils, Derek?

DEREK   No; not replace the pencils. Re-place the pencils. Reposition them.

TOM   Oh; re-place the pencils. Why's that?

DEREK   Well, *(picking up a pencil)* you see, you've placed the pencil to the right of the paper.

TOM   Yes.

DEREK   So, you've assumed everyone is right-handed.

TOM   Have I?

DEREK Oh, yes. You've shown bias towards the right-handed members of our Committee.

TOM Have I?

DEREK Oh, yes. Equality at all times, Tom. You should know that, being a police officer.

TOM Oh, I do know that, Derek.

DEREK Good.

TOM But, I wasn't intentionally showing bias.

DEREK No?

TOM No. I was actually showing that I believed everyone was physically capable of picking up a pencil where ever it was. That those left-handed members of our committee were physically capable of reaching across a piece of paper to pick up a pencil.

DEREK Ah, you see, you used the word physically twice then, Tom. Bias against the disabled as well as the left-handed.

TOM Hang on, Derek, this is getting silly. No one on the committee is either left-handed or disabled.

DEREK Now you're making assumptions. You should never assume things, Tom. To assume is to make an ass out of u and me!

TOM *(trying to make sense of what's just been said)* What? *(Trying to remain calm)* I'm not making assumptions, Derek. I know that none of the committee are disabled or left-handed!

DEREK *(dismissing Tom's comments with a wave of his hand)* Place the pencils here *(he moves the pencils to the spoon position)* and we show no bias.

TOM I wasn't showing any bias.

DEREK   *(holding up a pencil)* That's why they're sharpened at each end. To show no bias.

TOM   I wasn't showing any.... Oh, never mind!

DEREK   *(moving more pencils and not looking up)* What's that?

TOM   Nothing. I'll go and help Sarah in the kitchen. *(He exits to the kitchen)*

DEREK   Ok. *(He continues to fuss round the table, straightening chairs etc.)*

Marjorie enters, fiddling with her ear

DEREK   *(not looking up as he is doing his usual fussing)* Evening, Marjorie.

Marjorie continues to fiddle with her ear without answering

(Not getting a response, Derek looks up at Marjorie) Evening, Marjorie.

MARJORIE   Sorry, Derek?

DEREK   I said evening, Marjorie.

MARJORIE   Oh, sorry, Derek. Evening.

DEREK   You alright?

MARJORIE   Me? Oh yes, fine, thank you.

DEREK   Good. It's just that you didn't seem to hear me when I said hello to you the first, and indeed, the second time.

MARJORIE   Pardon?

DEREK   Oh good grief. *(Raising his voice)* Is your hearing ok? Do you have a new hearing aid?

MARJORIE   Sorry, Derek. I can't really hear you. I'm struggling with this new hearing aid.

DEREK   I thought as much.

MARJORIE   Pardon?

DEREK   *(raising his voice more)* I said I thought as much. Hang on. *(He picks up a pencil, decides it's not up to the job, so finds a marker pen and piece of paper and writes 'Can you turn it up?' on it and shows it to Marjorie)*

MARJORIE   *(reading it)* Oh, yes. It's a new-fangled one. I have to move my head to the side, like this *(she demonstrates by shaking her head sideways quite vigorously)* and the volume increases incrementally.

DEREK   Looks lethal to me.

MARJORIE   Sorry?

DEREK   ~~*(raising his voice again)* I said, oh, hang on.~~ *(He writes 'Shake your head!')*

MARJORIE   ~~*(reading)* Why should I shake my head?~~

DEREK   ~~*(starting to lose his cool. Shouting)* To raise the vol~~ume.

MARJORIE   ~~Oh I see! Right. Ok. Well~~. I'm not very good at this. Erm, so I know whether the volume is going up or down can you talk to me, Derek, whilst I move my head. Then I'll be able to tell.

DEREK   Do I have to?

MARJORIE   ~~Pard~~on?

DEREK   Oh my.... *(Writing 'And say what?!')*

MARJORIE   ~~Oh I don't mind. How about this evening's agenda~~?

DEREK   ~~Ok~~.

MARJORIE   Pardon.

45

DEREK *(shouting)* Ok! *(He starts to read the agenda.)*

Throughout the following Marjorie vigorously shakes her head to one side then the other. Pausing occasionally to listen to Derek before fine tuning the volume with more head shakes

　　　　　　　　Tonight's agenda is for a special meeting to organise the teams and running order for this year's Village Games. In alphabetical order: Archery. Captain: Derek. Others: Wilf and Charlie. Bowls. Captain: Derek. Others: Tom and George. Darts. Captain: Derek. Others: None.

MARJORIE　Got it, Derek, got it.

DEREK　You sure?

MARJORIE　Oh, yes. I can hear you perfectly now.

DEREK　Thank goodness.

MARJORIE　I just have the other problem left to deal with.

DEREK　What's that?

MARJORIE　Every time I walk past the TV it changes channel. It's driving Malcolm potty!

DEREK　~~What the!~~?

Tom and Sarah enter from the kitchen

TOM　Everything alright, Derek?

DEREK　Fine, thank you, Tom.

TOM　It's just that we heard shouting. We were going to come in, but I was changing the bulb in the kitchen and Sarah was holding the ladder for me.

DEREK　We're fine. It's just that Marjorie's got a new hearing aid.

TOM *(raising his voice and enunciating)* You've got a new hearing aid, have you, Marjorie? Having trouble with it, are we?

MARJORIE *(replying quietly)* It's fine now, thank you, Tom.

Sarah laughs at Tom

TOM *(embarrassed)* Oh, right, sorry. Thought you were still struggling.

MARJORIE No, fine now. It just has a tricky way of adjusting the volume, that's all.

DEREK Don't ask her to demonstrate. It'll give you a headache and her a concussion!

MARJORIE Thank you, Derek. I can hear you now!

DEREK Oh, yes, sorry, Marjorie.

Tyler and Tia enter. Holding hands

TYLER Hi, everyone.

TOM Evening, Tyler. Tia.

TIA Hi.

MARJORIE Hello. I'll pop the urn on.

SARAH It's ok, Marjorie, I've already done it. Hi, Tia.

MARJORIE Oh, lovely, Sarah. Thank you.

DEREK Right. Let's get started.

TYLER Ah, yes, extra meeting for the Village Games.

DEREK That's correct.

TYLER   Just tell us which sports you're not participating in, Derek, rather than the ones you are. That'll make the meeting shorter!

Tia giggles

MARJORIE   Not helpful, Tyler.

TYLER   Quite right, Mrs Carter. Sorry. Sorry, Derek.

MARJORIE   Although I do think I'll allow myself to open the emergency rations biscuit tin tonight. *(She exits to the kitchen)*

Everyone takes their seats around the table as lights fade to blackout

Scene 2

Lights up on:
The same. A few days later. 2pm. Tom is sat at the table fiddling with a small electronic device. Sarah enters the hall. She's not being quiet on purpose, but when she sees Tom so engrossed in his work she creeps up behind him.

SARAH *(quite loudly)* 'Ello, 'ello, 'ello! What's going on 'ere then?!

TOM *(during the above, Tom jumps out of his chair with fright)* Jeeesus, Sarah! What are you trying to do to me?

SARAH Whoops, sorry, Tom. I didn't think you'd react like that!

TOM How on earth did you think I'd react?

SARAH I don't know really. Sorry.

TOM You really shouldn't creep around like that.

SARAH *(sitting down next to Tom)* And you, Mr Policeman, should lock the door when you're in here on your own. You know the rules.

TOM That's after dark. Not at this time of day.

SARAH Yes; why are you here at this time of day?

TOM *(holding up the electronic device)* Just checking the cameras and mics.

SARAH Have you managed to catch Giuseppe and Tyler on them yet?

TOM I don't think so.

SARAH You don't think so? Surely you either have or you haven't.

TOM Well; we have picked up images and words.

49

SARAH	I should hope so. There're classes and groups in here most days.
TOM	But there seems to be glitches.
SARAH	What do you mean 'glitches?'
TOM	Well, the footage seems to be clear, both sound and vision, and then one or the other or both stop working for a bit and then start again.
SARAH	How strange.
TOM	And what's even more strange is that it seems to be whenever Marjorie is near the equipment!
SARAH	Really?
TOM	Yes. Marjorie comes in to view, or gets picked up by a mic, and as she gets closer – poof – no sound or vision. Then she moves away and….
SARAH	Poof – she's back again?
TOM	Exactly!
SARAH	How bizarre.
TOM	Yes, well, anyway. We don't think Giuseppe and Tyler have been back here yet. So I thought I'd pop in and adjust the settings. See if we can Marjorie-proof them!
SARAH	Sounds a good idea. Bit dangerous sitting there doing that, isn't it Tom? What if I'd been Giuseppe or Tyler creeping in?
TOM	That's why I'm here now. They're both at work. Other officers are tracking them.
SARAH	Oh, ok.
TOM	Talking of this time of day; what are you doing up here?

SARAH	Oh, I *(faltering)* thought I'd bring some clean tea towels up....
TOM	Right and where are they?
SARAH	What?
TOM	The tea towels?
SARAH	*(looking around)* Oh, I, er, left them at home!
TOM	You came all the way up here with some clean tea towels which you left at home.
SARAH	Er, yes, that's it!
TOM	And now the truth, Sarah, please. What's going on?
SARAH	Oh, Tom. I'm sorry. I just had to see you.
TOM	What about?
SARAH	Nothing.
TOM	Nothing?
SARAH	Yes, I didn't want to see you about anything..... I just wanted to *see* you.
TOM	Sorry. You've lost me.
SARAH	I just like to see you.... Look at you. That's all.
TOM	*(slightly embarrassed)* You've been stalking me?
SARAH	No, not stalking you. That's a far too strong word.
TOM	I am a police officer, Sarah. I do know what stalking is when I see it.

Sarah bows her head in shame

(Taking her hand) I thought you said you loved me?

51

SARAH	*(looking up at Tom)* Oh, I do. I do love you.
TOM	But; stalking isn't the action of someone who's in love, is it?
SARAH	It is, if the love isn't reciprocated.
TOM	I love you as a friend. Isn't that enough?
SARAH	Frankly, no.
TOM	So; this stalking is your idea of real love, is it?
SARAH	That's not fair, Tom.
TOM	And stalking me is?
SARAH	Will you please stop calling it stalking?
TOM	Ok. You've been following me, then?
SARAH	That's a bit better.
TOM	How long for?
SARAH	About 15 minutes.
TOM	15 minutes?
SARAH	Today.
TOM	Oh, I see. 15 minutes today. What about before today?
SARAH	About three years.
TOM	*(letting go of her hand. Incredulously)* What?! Three years?!
SARAH	Yes.
TOM	And you don't want me to call it stalking?! *(Pause)* Do you know how that makes me feel?

SARAH	Wanted?
TOM	Abused.
SARAH	Oh, come on, Tom. Abused? No harm's been done.
TOM	No harm?! I've just found out you've been stalking me for three years and you say no harm's been done!
SARAH	The way you say three years makes it sound like I've been doing it constantly for three years. It's been on and off you know.
TOM	Ok, how often have you *followed* me?
SARAH	Oh, I don't know, once or twice a week.
TOM	Once or twice a week! I really could have you arrested for this. Stalking a police officer.
SARAH	Go on. *(Presenting her wrists to Tom)* Put the handcuffs on then.
TOM	*(lightening up a bit at this)* No, I won't. 'Coz that's what you want, don't you?
SARAH	Might be.
TOM	Look. If you want to see me, then see me. Just, don't follow me. Please.
SARAH	Ok. Sorry. Can I go now, Mr Policeman?
TOM	*(smiling)* Yes. Go on.
SARAH	*(heading towards the exit)* Thanks for not arresting me.
TOM	Go on. Get out of here before I change my mind.
SARAH	Make sure you lock up and give the key back to Derek, like a good policeman.

TOM If you don't go pretty sharpish I'll get my truncheon out.

SARAH Promises, promises! *(She blows Tom a kiss)* Bye.

TOM Bye. *(Sarah exits) (Picking up the electronic device and turning a screwdriver in it)* Now, then, Marjorie. Let's see if you can get past this! *(He gives the screwdriver one more large turn)*

Lights fade to blackout

Scene 3

Lights up on:
The same. A Wednesday evening a couple of months later, 7:15pm.
Derek is busying himself around the table, placing the pencils and paper in front of each seat in his usual manner.

DEREK *(talking to himself whilst holding a pencil up to the light)* I really wish that playgroup would stick to their own cupboard and their own *coloured* pencils. Blunt. *(He puts the pencil down and picks up another)* Blunt. Oh, this is intolerable.

Sarah and Tom enter

SARAH Hi, Derek.

TOM Evening, Derek.

DEREK Ah, Sarah, Tom. Evening. You don't happen to have a pencil sharpener on you, do you? Either of you?

SARAH A pencil sharpener?

DEREK Yes. *(Holding up another pencil)* Damn playgroup's been in my cupboard again. Look.

SARAH Oh, dear. I'm afraid I don't have a pencil sharpener on me, Derek. Not something I usually have a need for.

TOM *(patting his pockets just to make a gesture, rather than really checking for one)* Me neither, Derek.

DEREK But you're a policeman, Tom. Surely you always carry a….. Oh, hang on. I think I might have one in the car. Excuse me a minute, won't you?! *(He dashes out of the hall)*

TOM Sure. *(He watches him leave)* Pencil sharpener!

SARAH I can't believe he's got one in his car.

TOM Can't you? I can!

Sarah laughs

Pause

SARAH So you've done it, then?

TOM Done what?

SARAH Got some evidence against Giuseppe? From your hidden devices? *(She points and looks randomly around the hall)* Wherever they are.

TOM Oh, loads. Clear pictures and sound.

SARAH What about poor young Tyler. Is he in it up to his neck as well?

TOM He's in it deep, but maybe not up to his neck. We've got legal people looking into it. Giuseppe's definitely in trouble. He's clearly got a hold over Tyler. That might be enough to save him. We'll have to wait and see.

SARAH What now?

TOM Just got to wait for the go ahead from the DCI. Other officers are still compiling a case against the inside man and Spencer.

SARAH Ok.

TOM Come on. Let's get that urn on. I haven't had a cuppa since breakfast.

They both exit to the kitchen. Derek re-enters holding a pencil sharpener

DEREK I knew it. I knew I had one somewhere. *(He starts to sharpen a pencil)* Once a scout, always a scout!

After a few moments Marjorie enters and stands just inside the door

MARJORIE Evening, Derek.

DEREK *(looking up)* Oh, good evening, Marjorie. How are you?

Marjorie holds her hand up as to stop Derek talking. She then vigorously shakes her head three times to one side

MARJORIE   Say again!

DEREK   I said good evening, Marjorie. How *(Marjorie puts her hand up to stop him again. She does one more nod and waves Derek on)* How are you?

MARJORIE   *(walking towards the table as if nothing untoward had just happened)* Fine, thank you, Derek. How are you?

DEREK   Very well, thank you.

MARJORIE   Last month's minutes ok?

DEREK   Yes, spot on, Marjorie. Thank you.

MARJORIE   Good. I think it's this new hearing aid, you know. I'm finding taking the minutes themselves much easier now. Everything's so much clearer.

DEREK   Yes, well, good. But your spelling and punctuation has improved as well.

MARJORIE   Yes, well, so it should. It was a very expensive hearing aid! *(She exits to the kitchen)*

Derek stands, hands on hips, shaking his head, not knowing what to make of that last comment. He starts to straighten chairs etc. again

Tia and Tyler enter

TYLER   Hi, Derek.

DEREK   *(looking up)* Oh, hello, Tyler.

TIA   Hi.

DEREK   Tia.

TYLER   All ready for the Games, then? Three days to go!

DEREK Oh, yes. All ready here. You got your boys ready for the five-a-side?

TYLER Yes. Good training last night. We're up for it!

DEREK Excellent. That's what I like to hear!

TIA And Tyler beat Giuseppe at darts twice at the weekend, didn't you?

TYLER Yep.

DEREK Yes, well, well done, but I'm still playing on Saturday.

TYLER Yes, I know that. Tia brought it up so you'd know that Giuseppe is beatable. That's all. Give you some confidence.

TIA That's all.

DEREK Oh, right. Ok. Good. *(Pause)* Thank you.

TYLER You're welcome. *(Patting Derek on the shoulder)* We're all on the same side, aren't we?

DEREK Yes. *(Slight smile appearing)* Yes, we are.

TIA Lovely!

Marjorie, Sarah and Tom enter from the kitchen carrying trays of teas etc between them

DEREK Ah! There you all are. Shall we begin?

The teas are passed around and seats are taken. Marjorie sits at one end of the table near to one of the pot plants

TOM Yes, but before we do, and before Laura arrives for the KADS, I just thought I'd mention that there's been a death in her family.

MARJORIE Oh, no. Sorry to hear that.

DEREK Anyone we know?

TOM Erm, no. We went up to the In-Laws for the weekend and nothing was mentioned on the Friday night. We slept quite well on the new bed they'd got and then they told us about it on the Saturday morning. *(Pause)* Brutus has died.

MARJORIE Oh, dear.

TIA Oh, no.

DEREK And you didn't notice his casket in your room on the Friday night?

TOM No, we didn't, Derek.

DEREK Things are looking up then. Where had they put it?

TOM We didn't notice it because we were sleeping on it.

Silence

DEREK You what?!

TOM That nice new bed had a nice new base. Filled with the ashes of Brutus!

Tyler and Tia start to laugh. Sarah places her hand on Tom's in support whilst stifling laughter

MARJORIE Oh dear, that's made me feel quite queezy!

DEREK Ah, well, erm, not a lot you can say to that, is there?

TOM No, not really, Derek. I just thought you'd like to know.

DEREK Yes, well, commiserations, Tom. *(Pause)* Right then, first things first. Saturday's refreshments. Marjorie; you're in here with the teas and sandwiches and stuff, aren't you?

MARJORIE Yes, I am.

SARAH　　　　And I'm helping her, Derek.

DEREK　　　　Are you Sarah? Oh, that's lovely. Thank you. Erm, unfortunately I went around to those new people at 42 and they aren't Bakers, well they are, but they're not, so you're going to have to use your usual suppliers Marjorie, if that's ok?

MARJORIE　　Yes, that's fine, Derek. *(Marjorie starts to shake her head slightly and put her finger in her ear)*

DEREK　　　　You alright, Marjorie? *(No response)* Do you need another volume check?

MARJORIE　　Eh? Oh, no.

DEREK　　　　What's wrong, then?

MARJORIE　　I'm not sure. Ever since I've sat down I've been feeling a little pain in my ear.

SARAH　　　　The one with the new hearing aid in?

MARJORIE　　Yes. A little interference as well. And I think I just picked up a trace of Radio 2!

DEREK　　　　Really?

MARJORIE　　Yes, I think it was the travel news. Sounds like there's been a nasty accident on the M1. Junction 24a, I believe.

TIA　　　　　Oh dear.

They all glance at Tia

　　　　　　　　Sorry.

DEREK　　　　What can be causing it, do you think?

MARJORIE　　Well, it's done it occasionally before. Near electronic devices.

Tom and Sarah exchange troubled glances

DEREK No electronic devices in this old hall, Marjorie.

MARJORIE Really? Nothing?

DEREK Nothing. No wi-fi. Not even a hi-fi!

TYLER *(getting his mobile phone out of his pocket)* Even the phone signal's really weak, Mrs Carter.

MARJORIE But it's since I sat down. *(Turning around)* What's this plant?

More exchanged glances between Tom and Sarah

DEREK Just a plant, Marjorie. It's been there for years.

MARJORIE I know. But, why is it affecting me now? *(She starts to poke around the plant)*

DEREK It can't be. It's just a plant.

TOM *(deciding to step in to divert the conversation and to stop Marjorie poking around the plant)* Well, it could be.

DEREK Really?

TOM Yes. I was reading the other day about increased photosynthesis activity being recorded in certain houseplants at certain times of the year.

MARJORIE Really?

DEREK Well I never!

Tyler looks suspiciously at Tom

TOM And maybe it's this plant's turn.

Everyone's staring at the plant

MARJORIE   Amazing.

TOM   And that this can give off tiny amounts of static. *(Standing up)* I tell you what, Marjorie, swap seats with me.

MARJORIE   Yes, ok, Tom. *(They swap seats)*

TOM   Better?

MARJORIE   *(feeling her ear)* Yes. Yes, it is, Thank you.

TOM   *(exchanging glances with Sarah)* No problem.

DEREK   Right. Well, then. Now we've got comfy and had a travel update we can carry on. Now then, the football tournament will kick off first as there're quite a few games to fit in. The bowls will start a little later and....

During the above the lights fade to blackout

Scene 4

Lights up on:
The same. 8:55pm. Laura enters. She's as dizzy as before. Carrying CD/cassette player and bag of scripts etc.

DEREK *(immediately jumping up and offering Laura his seat)* Ah! Here she is! Our very own Sofia Coppola!

LAURA *(accepting the seat)* Oh, thank you, Derek.

SARAH Found another female director then, have we, Derek?

DEREK Needs must, Sarah, needs must.

LAURA Ah, that's very kind of you to go to the trouble, Derek.

DEREK No trouble at all, Laura.

TYLER No trouble if you *have* wi-fi, eh, Derek?

DEREK I don't mind admitting in using the internet for research on the matter, Tyler. That's what it's there for.

TYLER True, true.

DEREK I shall probably use it again later to find out more about that photosynthesis static thing and that plant. *(Pointing at the pot plant)*

TOM Oh, I wouldn't bother with that, Derek.

DEREK Really? It sounded quite interesting to me.

TOM No. A bit technical and boring really.

DEREK Well, I might look into it after the Games are done. Too busy up until then.

TOM Good idea.

DEREK Right, well, I'll leave you in the capable hands of Ms Coppola and see you all on Saturday for the Games.

LAURA	Yes. Thank you, Derek. Goodnight.
TOM	Night.

Others talking over each other as Derek exits

MARJORIE	Night, night, Derek.
TYLER	See ya.
SARAH	Goodnight.
TIA	Bye.

Everyone settles down for the KADS meeting

LAURA	He seemed in a good mood tonight.
MARJORIE	Yes.
TIA	Well, me and Tyler tried to boost his confidence for the Games.
LAURA	Really? Well done. How did you do that?
TYLER	We told him that Giuseppe had lost at darts a lot recently and that Derek has a good chance of beating him.
SARAH	And has he?
TIA	Nope, no chance.
TYLER	Giuseppe'll murder him!
~~LAURA~~	~~Really?~~
~~TIA~~	~~Really.~~
~~LAURA~~	~~Oh, dear.~~
TYLER	He got a nine darter the other day.

TOM ~~Really?~~

TYLER ~~Yep.~~

LAURA   I've no idea what that is, but it sounds very impressive.

TOM   It is, darling, it is.

LAURA   Oh, well, at least you've tried to help Derek.

SARAH   Yes, well done, you two.

MARJORIE Bless them. Such lovely young people.

Tom and Sarah exchange glances

TIA   Stop it, you're embarrassing us! Let's get on.

~~Daisy enters~~

LAURA   Yes, let's. *(Seeing Daisy)* ~~Ah, just in time, Daisy.~~ Excellent. I wanted to start tonight's rehearsal ~~with your duet with Tyler. Giuseppe not with you~~?

~~DAISY   Hi, everyone.~~

Cursory waves and smiles from the others in the direction of Daisy who is a little out of breath

          ~~Sorry I'm late. No.~~ No, Giuseppe. He just ~~texted me to~~ say he had some business to attend to and he ~~wouldn~~'t be able to ~~make it tonight.~~

Further glances between Tom and Sarah

          ~~He says sorry. That's why I'm late. I was expecting him to pick me up. Had to walk.~~

LAURA   Oh, well, never mind. It would be better with him, but we'll do bits he's not involved in.

DAISY   Ok.

65

LAURA Right, before we begin, I just wanted to say that I've just had written confirmation from the theatre. So, it's all go for three nights rehearsal and three shows on the dates we requested!

Over one another

TOM Great, love.

MARJORIE Wonderful.

SARAH Lovely.

LAURA Giuseppe can be rather persuasive, can't he Tia.

TIA Yes. Usually when he wants something!

LAURA ~~Yes, and I gave him something.~~

TOM Sorry, darling; you gave him something?

LAURA Yes.

TOM What did you give him, love?

LAURA The show at the theatre of course. What did you think I gave him?

TOM ~~I'm not sure, love.~~

LAURA Putting the show on at the theatre. That's what he wanted and that's what I've given him!

TOM *(exchanging glances with Sarah)* Right, love. Of course.

LAURA Right. Tyler a~~nd Daisy~~. Your duet then. With music for the first time. *(She points at the CD player)* Now remember; this is Carl recalling how he felt the first time he saw Bella and how she initially shunned him, before falling in love with him. Ok?

TYLER Yes.

LAURA	The verses are all yours, Tyler. The choruses are the duet bits, ok?
~~TYLER~~	~~Sure.~~
~~DAISY~~	~~Ok.~~
LAURA	Now then, *(she starts to position Tyler ~~and Daisy~~ as she talks)* you start by standing here *(she positions Daisy in front of the table near to the exit to the kitchen)* and you here. *(Tyler is positioned in front of the table in the centre of the hall)* As the song progresses I want you to make your way across towards ~~Daisy,~~ Tyler, but only when I say so.
~~TYLER~~	~~Ok.~~
LAURA	You eventually embrace. Is that ok?
~~TYLER~~	~~Fine.~~
~~DAISY~~	~~Fine.~~
TIA	Do they have to?
LAURA	Have to what, Tia?
TIA	Embrace.
LAURA	Well, it is a love story.
TYLER	It's just a hug. An acting hug at that.
TIA	I know, honey. I just don't like seeing you hugging other girls. That's all.
~~DAISY~~	~~You don't like it?! What do you think Giuseppe's gonna make of us hugging?~~
TIA	Oh, yes. It's not just the bad singing that runs in the family; it's the jealousy as well!
TYLER	Oh, well, er, maybe we should leave out the hug.

LAURA Don't be silly, Tyler. It's a love story and a love song. ~~Giuseppe will be alright. I'll take him to one side and have a quiet 'tête á tête' with him.~~

TOM ~~Did you say 'tête á tête', darling?~~

LAURA ~~Yes.~~

TOM ~~Ok. Just checking.~~

Sarah smiles

LAURA Right then. Positions and I'll press play.

Laura presses play and the introduction of 'Now or Never (If the Game is to be Won)' plays – this song is an original piece of music written for this play. CD and music are available (see front of book for details)

TYLER *(standing a reasonable distance from Daisy starts to sing)*
I OPENED MY EYES,
AND WHAT DID I SEE BUT YOU.
WAS IT A DREAM OR TRUE?
SPARKLING LIKE BRAND NEW.

LAURA *(raising her voice over the music)* Move a bit closer, please, Tyler.

TYLER *(stepping forward as he sings the second verse)*
YOU GLANCED ACROSS
THE OPEN FLOOR AT ME,
WHAT COULD IT BE,
THAT HAD KEPT US BOTH APART.

LAURA *(raising her voice again)* And chorus together.

TYLER & DAISY FOR IT IS NOW OR NEVER
IF THE GAME IS TO BE WON.
YOU EITHER GAMBLE IT ALL,
OR TURN AWAY AND RUN.

LAURA Closer Tyler.

TYLER *(moving a little closer)*
I DECIDED TO RISK IT
AND ADVANCED TOWARDS YOU.
WHAT COULD YOU DO,
BUT STAND AND LISTEN TO ME.

LAURA And now almost within Daisy's reach, Tyler.

TYLER *(moving once more)*
YOU LOOKED AT ME, TRIUMPHANTLY,
AS IF I WERE A CREATURE.
YOU DISAPPEARED AND I THOUGHT NEITHER OF US
WOULD HAVE A FUTURE.

LAURA Step apart.

TYLER & DAISY *(doing so)*
FOR IT IS NOW OR NEVER
IF THE GAME IS TO BE WON.
YOU EITHER GAMBLE IT ALL,
OR TURN AWAY AND RUN.

LAURA Ok. Eight bars of instrumental. During this next verse, I want you to make your way towards her please, Tyler and grab her! The passion must build through the last chorus and the long coda.

TYLER *(nodding at Laura and doing so)*
I GAMBLED IT ALL
IT WAS HER WHO TOOK TO HER HEELS,
I SUPPOSE IT WAS NO BIG DEAL.
MAYBE I'LL GET ANOTHER CHANCE.

LAURA And hold hands

TYLER & DAISY *(doing so)*
BUT IT IS NOW OR NEVER
IF THE GAME IS TO BE WON.
YOU EITHER GAMBLE IT ALL,
OR TURN AWAY AND RUN.

LAURA Now, embrace!

The 16-bar coda plays out as Tyler and Daisy hold each other extremely close. The music ends. They separate. Everyone applauds

LAURA *(pressing stop)* Well done, ~~you two~~. Very good first try ~~with the music.~~

~~**DAISY** Thank you.~~

~~**TYLER** Thanks. *(Turning to Tia)* That alright, love?~~

~~**TIA** I suppose so. As long as she's only getting an acting hug, then you can give me a proper hug!~~

~~**TYLER** Ok. Come here. *(Tyler and Tia hug)*~~

~~**SARAH** Aah. Sweet.~~

LAURA ~~Right.~~ We'll try that song again next week, ~~if you don't mind.~~

TYLER We can't, Laura.

LAURA Why not?

TYLER Me and Tia are going on holiday next Monday. Two weeks in Tenerife.

LAURA Oh, yes. You did tell me. I forgot.

TIA Sorry.

LAURA No need to apologise, Tia. Everyone deserves a holiday. It's just that I don't think we're gonna get that song perfect with the amount of rehearsals we've got left; especially if we take two weeks out for your holiday.

TYLER Oh.

LAURA I know. I've just had a thought. We're all here on Saturday for the Village Games. How about I bring the CD player along and we grab five minutes in here in the afternoon to try it once or twice.

TYLER	We'll be a bit busy, with all the events going on.
LAURA	I know; but if I've got the CD player we can do it any time we get a chance. Ok?
TYLER	Ok.
~~DAISY~~	~~Fine by me.~~
LAURA	Lovely. Now I'd like to try the scene when Carl's grandmother, Marjorie, meets Bella's mother and father for the first time. I think we really need to work on the tension in that scene.

During the above the lights fade to blackout

Scene 5

Lights up on:
The same. Three days later. Day of the Village Games. 6:00pm.
Marjorie and Sarah are busying themselves clearing the table of cups etc.
The day is clearly coming to an end. Derek enters wearing his tracksuit.
He looks flustered and sweaty. He is followed by Tyler and Tia. They're
both also wearing sporty attire.

TIA You shouldn't have done that, Derek.

DEREK I know I shouldn't.

TYLER All you've managed to do with that stunt is rile him.

DEREK I know, I know.

TYLER Rile him just before the darts match.

DEREK Yes, yes, I know!

MARJORIE What have you done, Derek?

DEREK Nothing!

MARJORIE It doesn't sound like nothing.

TIA ~~It's not nothing, Mrs Carter. Tell her what you did, Derek.~~

DEREK ~~*(getting grumpier)* You tell her.~~

TIA ~~No, you did it, Derek, you tell her.~~

DEREK ~~Huh!~~

TIA ~~*(becoming forceful)* If you don't tell her I'll change sides and support my brother!~~

DEREK ~~You wouldn't do that, would you, Tia?~~

TIA ~~I would, in fact I will if you… you don't man up and tell Marjorie what you've done. *(Pause)* Well~~?

72

DEREK Alright, alright. I'll tell her. *(Pause)*

MARJORIE *(quietly)* What have you done, Derek?

DEREK *(head down, muttering)* I threw his tracksuit top into the oak tree.

MARJORIE *(putting her finger to her ear)* Pardon.

TIA Marjorie can't hear you, Derek. Say it again louder for her.

DEREK *(a little louder)* Tell her to shake her head….

TIA No, Derek, it's not her hearing aid it's you. Say it louder so that both Marjorie and Sarah can hear it.

DEREK Alright. *(Loudly, blurting)* I threw Giuseppe's tracksuit top into the oak tree. Ok?

Sarah starts to laugh

MARJORIE Oh, dear, Derek. Why did you do that?

DEREK Because he said it again.

MARJORIE He didn't?

DEREK He did!

MARJORIE The same thing as last year.

DEREK Yes.

MARJORIE Exactly the same?

DEREK Exactly the same.

MARJORIE Oh, dear.

DEREK Oh, dear, exactly. I know you said last year it was sporting banter. But to say the same thing again;

	exactly the same thing again meant, it wasn't sporting banter. So, I had to act.
MARJORIE	And it sounds like you did.
DEREK	Well, he'd left his stupid Spencer-sponsored tracksuit top on a chair so I strode past him, picked it up and launched it into the oak tree.
MARJORIE	Ah.
SARAH	Has he got it back down, yet?
DEREK	No.
MARJORIE	Good.
SARAH	Really, Marjorie?
MARJORIE	Yes, really. If he's said the same to Derek as he did last year, then he deserves it.
SARAH	But what *did* he say?
DEREK	*(clearing his throat)* I'd rather not say.
SARAH	Oh. Right. That bad, eh?
DEREK	*(slumping into a chair)* Yes.
TYLER	The thing is, Derek, you've riled him before the darts match. Not a good thing to do.
DEREK	I know. Doesn't matter. We can't win the Games anyway.

During the above Tom enters wearing his bowls whites

TOM	Yes we can.
DEREK	*(looking up)* You what! How?

TOM	I've just won my bowls match which means we're one point ahead with the darts and table tennis to go.
DEREK	Really?
TOM	Yep. Malcolm's just put the score on the board. It's all official.
DEREK	But when I left the bowling green you were 1 set down and 3 down with only one end to go.
TOM	I know. But I got a 4 in the final end and won the tie-break! *(He beams)*
SARAH	Well done, Tom.
~~TOM~~	~~Thank you.~~
~~TIA~~	~~That's brilliant, Tom.~~
~~TOM~~	~~*(bowing)* I thank you!~~
DEREK	*(sitting more upright)* So, one point ahead. I win the darts; the table tennis becomes a dead rubber and we win!
TOM	Yep!
DEREK	*(jumping up)* Brilliant! I'll just get my darts from the kitchen. *(He exits to the kitchen)*

Laura enters the hall carrying her CD player etc

LAURA	Ah. Here you are, Tyler. If we can just find Daisy we can have a go at your duet.
TYLER	I don't think now's the right time, Laura.
LAURA	Why not. We just need to get Daisy in here, try the song and go home. I've been lugging this thing *(pointing at the CD player which she's placed on the table)* around all day trying to get you two together and this is our last chance.

TYLER	But they're just about to play the darts.
LAURA	Well, they play it in here, don't they?
TYLER	Yes.
LAURA	Good. You can watch while you sing.
TOM	Is that going to work, love?
SARAH	Hardly.
LAURA	*(glaring at Sarah)* Please. Just one try. Then I can go home and mark that huge pile of school books I have sitting there. Ok? *(She starts to look through her bag for something)*
TOM	Alright, love. Keep calm. *(Looking at Tyler)* Just one sing through, please, Tyler? For my own sanity!
TYLER	Ok, Tom. Just one.
LAURA	*(still fumbling through her bag)* Lovely, thank you. Now if I can just find that CD....

Giuseppe enters the hall followed by Daisy. He is without his tracksuit top and is fuming

GIUSEPPE	Where is he?
MARJORIE	Who?
GIUSEPPE	You know who.
MARJORIE	He's in the kitchen.
GIUSEPPE	Right! *(He starts to stride towards the kitchen)*
TOM	*(moving to block his way)* I don't think so, Giuseppe.
GIUSEPPE	What?
TOM	You're not going in there whilst you're in that mood.

GIUSEPPE	Move aside, Tom.
TOM	I may be out of uniform, but I suggest you calm down and move away from me before you find yourself in difficulties.
~~DAISY~~	~~(grabbing Giuseppe's arm) Come on, Zep. It's just a tracksuit top.~~
~~GIUSEPPE~~	~~I know. But it's the principle. Isn't it?~~
MARJORIE	You know what you said to him again, Giuseppe. Two years you've now said that to him. I think you got off very lightly, don't you?
GIUSEPPE	*(starting to calm down)* Yes. I guess so.
~~TOM~~	~~Alright, now?~~
~~GIUSEPPE~~	~~Yes, sorry, Tom.~~
~~TOM~~	~~Right.~~

Derek enters from the kitchen fiddling with his darts

DEREK	*(looking at his darts)* I must get that drawer fixed. I put my darts in there this morning and the damn thing got jammed. *(Looking up and seeing Giuseppe. Taking a step back)* Ah, now then, Giuseppe, your tracksuit top. Er. Sorry about that, but er, what you said wasn't particularly pleasant.

Daisy elbows Giuseppe to encourage him to join in the peace process

GIUSEPPE	Yes, well, I suppose I shouldn't have said that. Sorry. It's just a tracksuit top.
TOM	Good. Well done.
DEREK	Have you managed to get it down yet? Your tracksuit top?

GIUSEPPE	Not yet. I've left the basketball team forming a pyramid.
DEREK	Oh, right, well, if that doesn't work I'll bring up my long ladder and maybe we can get it down together.
GIUSEPPE	Ok.

Both Giuseppe and Derek step forward and share a brief hand shake

TOM	Right. Darts. Where's the dartboard, Derek?
DEREK	*(pointing off stage towards the exit)* Just there, Tom. Next to the door.
TOM	I told you last year that I wasn't too keen on it being next to the door. It's a bit dangerous. Health and safety and all that.
GIUSEPPE	Not when we're playing, Tom. We're far too accurate, aren't we, Derek?
DEREK	Yes. Far too accurate.
TOM	Yes, well, be careful.
GIUSEPPE	Right. I gather we're one point behind with just the darts and the table tennis left, right?
DEREK	Right.
GIUSEPPE	Excellent. All to play for then!

Laura has spent all this time fumbling through her bag

LAURA	Got it! *(She produces the CD)*
TOM	What's that, love?
LAURA	The CD for the song. Ready Tyler, Daisy?
DAISY	Oh.

TYLER	Erm.
DEREK	What's this?
LAURA	We're just going to have a quick sing of a song that's in my play.
DEREK	Now?
LAURA	Yes, now.
DEREK	But we're about to play darts. Can't you wait.
LAURA	*(frustrated)* I've been waiting all day, Derek. I am a teacher with loads of work at home and I've been following Daisy with the netball and Tyler with the football all day long and now they're in the same room they will sing for me *(losing it)* so I can go home! Ok?
TOM	*(looking pleadingly at Derek whilst comforting Laura)* It's alright love, it's alright.
GIUSEPPE	Come on Derek. We can play whilst they sing. We're used to playing darts with lots of noise going on, aren't we?
DEREK	Yes, I suppose so.
DAISY	Oi, it's not noise. It's singing and me and Tyler sound good together, don't we?
TYLER	I guess so.
GIUSEPPE	*(staring threateningly at Tyler)* As long as you're not *too* good together.
TOM	Right, chaps, I'll score.

Tom walks towards the exit, out of sight, next to the unseen dartboard

LAURA	Right; positions please, Daisy and Tyler. *(They respond)* As much passion as we can muster this time, please both of you.

On the word 'passion' Giuseppe glances over his shoulder at Tyler and Daisy. Laura presses play on the CD player. As the 17-bar intro starts, Derek and Giuseppe have 3 practice darts each. Then....

TOM (*off stage, over the music intro*) Nearest bull to start.

Derek throws one dart

TOM (*off stage*) Bull. *(Derek retrieves his dart)*

Giuseppe throws one dart

TOM (*off stage*) 25. *(Giuseppe retrieves his dart as Derek clenches his fist at his first minor victory)* Derek to throw first.

*From now on the darts match goes in time with the song. Each dart is thrown in time with the music. The <u>underlined words</u> are when Derek must throw his darts, the **WORDS IN BOLD ITALICS** are when Giuseppe must throw his. Tom continues to call the score from offstage. Exactly two legs of darts fit into the song. The song is repeated exactly the same as earlier. Same actions and movement, but there are no interjections/comments from Laura.*
The first leg of darts, up until 'Game, Giuseppe' is called by Tom, is played normally. Both players start well, but Derek starts to fade under the pressure and his facial expressions must follow that as he berates himself during Giuseppe's throws.
The second leg starts evenly again, but this time Giuseppe is distracted by Tyler and Daisy getting closer to each other and eventually embracing.

TYLER I <u>O</u>PENED MY EYES,
AND <u>WHAT</u> DID I SEE BUT <u>YOU</u>. **TOM** 60
WAS IT A DREAM OR ***TRUE***?
SPARKLING LIKE BRAND ***NEW***. **TOM** 95

YOU <u>GLAN</u>CED ACROSS
THE <u>O</u>PEN FLOOR AT <u>ME</u>, **TOM** 85
WHAT COULD IT ***BE***,
THAT HAD ***KEPT*** US BOTH
    A***PAR***T. **TOM** 100

80

TYLER &	FOR IT IS <u>NOW</u> OR NEVER	
DAISY	IF THE <u>GAME</u> IS TO BE <u>WON</u>.	**TOM** 60
	YOU EITHER ***GAM***BLE IT ALL,	
	OR ***TURN*** AWAY AND ***RUN***.	**TOM** 100

TYLER	I DE<u>C</u>IDED TO RISK IT	
	AND AD<u>VAN</u>CED TOWARDS	
	YOU.	**TOM** 100
	WHAT COULD YOU ***DO***,	
	BUT ***STAND*** AND LISTEN TO ***ME***.	**TOM** 140

YOU <u>LOO</u>KED AT ME, TRI<u>UM</u>PHANTLY,
AS <u>IF</u> I WERE A CREATURE.   **TOM** 26
YOU ***DI***SAPPEARED AND I
    THOUGHT ***NEI***THER OF US
                TOM Game, Giuseppe.
WOULD HAVE A FUTURE.   2nd leg, Giuseppe
                to throw first.

TYLER &	FOR IT IS ***NOW*** OR NEVER	
DAISY	IF THE ***GAME*** IS TO BE ***WON***.	**TOM** 100
	YOU EITHER <u>GAM</u>BLE IT ALL,	
	OR <u>TURN</u> AWAY AND <u>RUN</u>.	**TOM** 60

8 bars of instrumental. Darts continue to be thrown in time with the music

3 darts from Giuseppe	**TOM** 60
3 darts from Derek	**TOM** 60

TYLER	I ***GAM***BLED IT ALL	
	IT WAS ***HER*** WHO TOOK TO HER	
	HEELS,	**TOM** 45
	I SUPPOSE IT WAS NO BIG <u>DEAL</u>.	
	<u>MAY</u>BE I'LL GET ANOTHER	
	<u>CHAN</u>CE.	**TOM** 100

TYLER &	BUT IT IS ***NOW*** OR NEVER	
DAISY	IF THE ***GAME*** IS TO BE ***WON***.	**TOM** 26
	YOU EITHER <u>GAM</u>BLE IT ALL,	
	OR <u>TURN</u> AWAY AND <u>RUN</u>.	**TOM** 100

16 bars ending. Darts continue to be thrown in time with the music

> *3 darts from Giuseppe who is losing it as he watches Tyler and Daisy embrace*

TOM 7

> *3 darts from Derek*

TOM 140

> *3 wild darts from Giuseppe who has now lost it completely*

TOM No score.

> *3 darts from Derek*

TOM Game, Derek.

As soon as Tom says 'Game, Derek' a furious Giuseppe thrusts his darts in his pocket and grabs Tyler, pulling him away from Daisy and raising his fist in the air as if to hit him

TIA *(shouting)* Stop, Zep.

SARAH No.

DAISY Zep, no!

TOM *(rushing over)* Think very carefully before you decide whether to finish that punch or not, Giuseppe.

Pause. Giuseppe slowly lowers his fist

DAISY *(grabbing hold of Giuseppe and pulling him away)* It's just acting, Zep. Just acting.

GIUSEPPE I know.

TYLER Sorry, man.

GIUSEPPE No, I'm sorry.

DAISY *(stroking his arm)* Just acting.

LAURA Well, all I can say is it was good acting and looking at Giuseppe's response, I'm not the only one who thought that!

GIUSEPPE *(calming down)* Yes. Good acting. Sorry, Laura.

LAURA *(moving towards Giuseppe and rubbing his other arm)* That's alright, love. You've had a stressful day like me, haven't you?

GIUSEPPE Erm.

DEREK Right; if you're all done, can we finish this darts match.

GIUSEPPE *(brushing off Daisy and more particularly Laura)* Yes, ok, Derek.

TOM *(moving back to the board)* Deciding leg. Derek to throw first.

Derek throws his 3 darts

TOM 100

Giuseppe throws his 3 darts

TOM 140

Derek throws

TOM 140

Giuseppe throws

TOM 140

Derek shakes his head before he throws

TOM 140

Giuseppe is really pumped up and throws

TOM 180 Derek you require 121

Derek takes precise aim and throws. Ooos and aahs all round as Derek misses a bullseye for the match

TOM 96 Giuseppe you require 41

Giuseppe only requires 2 darts for victory

DAISY Hurray! Well done!

Everyone else looks glum

GIUSEPPE Thanks, Daisy. *(Turning to Derek, shaking his hand)* Great game, Derek. Bad luck on that bull. You nearly had me.

DEREK Yes, well. Well done, Giuseppe. *(Derek slumps into the nearest chair)*

GIUSEPPE Let's go to the table tennis, Daisy.

TOM Wait a minute, Giuseppe.

GIUSEPPE What's up, Tom?

TOM I've just been given the signal from outside to play you this.

Tom takes a small remote control out of his pocket and points it into the air. He presses 'play' and voices are heard coming from a hidden speaker somewhere in the hall.

SARAH *(voice from recording)* 'Ello, 'ello, 'ello, what's going on 'ere then?

Everyone looks at Sarah who gives an embarrassed shrug

TOM *(stopping the recording)* Hang on, wrong bit.

He presses the button again

TOM *(voice from recording)* Poof! *(Trying to stop the recording, but to no avail)*

SARAH *(from recording)* Derek. *(Pause as Derek lifts up his head)* Poof!

Derek stands up looking at Tom and Sarah as Tom manages to stop the recording again

TOM Erm, sorry, Derek. Technical issues. Try this.

He presses the button again

SARAH *(from recording)* Put the handcuffs on.

Everyone stares at Sarah who now looks extremely embarrassed. Tom is thumping away at the remote trying to stop it, but to no avail

TOM *(from recording)* I'll get my truncheon out.

Everyone now looks at Tom who has managed to stop the recording

TOM *(looking around everyone)* Sorry about that. Sarah was just helping me with my equipment.

LAURA That's what it sounded like, darling.

TOM What, no, I mean my recording equipment, weren't you, Sarah?

SARAH Erm, yes.

TOM *(suddenly noticing Marjorie)* Hang on. Have you been sat there all the time, Marjorie?

MARJORIE Yes, dear. All the time. I've been entertained with darts, singing, fisticuffs and now your comedy and I haven't moved an inch!

TOM Well, that's it!

MARJORIE That's what?

TOM	That's why my playback isn't working. Why do you interfere with my electronic devices, Marjorie?
MARJORIE	Oh, am I dear. Sorry, I didn't think there were any electronic devices in here.
TOM	Well there are. Police devices.

Giuseppe starts to look towards the exit

	Stay where you are, Giuseppe.
MARJORIE	That'll be my hearing aid, Tom.
TOM	What? No, don't explain. Can you just change seats so I can get this playback sorted.
MARJORIE	*(moving seats)* Certainly, dear.

Tom holds up his remote and presses it again

GIUSEPPE	*(from recording)* We'll be breaking in the day after a big cash delivery, so our insider says.
TYLER	*(from recording)* Do you reckon six nights under that stage will be enough to get through?
GIUSEPPE	*(from recording)* Easily.

On this, Giuseppe looks around and moves rapidly out of the Village Hall. Tia jumps up in shock. Tom makes no effort to follow but Derek reacts by jumping up and swiftly throwing a dart out of the hall door

GIUSEPPE	*(as the dart hits him, probably in the backside)* Aagh!
DEREK	*(with a smile)* You know you're right, Tom. It is a bit dangerous having that dartboard next to the door.
TOM	There was no need for that, Derek. There are police officers out there.
DEREK	*(looking out)* What? Oh, yes. Sorry, Tom.

TIA	*(rushing over to Tom. Panicking)* What's happening, Tom. What's Zep done?
TOM	I think your boyfriend can probably answer that better than me.
TIA	*(to Tyler)* Tyler?

Tyler looks down

	What's going on, Tyler. *(Pause)* That was your voice on that recording, wasn't it? As well as Zep's?
TYLER	*(looking down)* Sorry, Tia.
TIA	What were you going to do, with Giuseppe?
TYLER	I only said I'd do it so as not to lose you.
TIA	What?
TOM	*(taking Tyler by the arm)* Come on Tyler. It'll all come out in the wash. Plenty of evidence to be ploughed through before verdicts are reached.

At this point Daisy jumps up and runs for the exit

SARAH	What's up with her?
LAURA	Maybe she's suddenly become concerned about Giuseppe?
TOM	Nope. She's the inside man!
TYLER	What?
DEREK	*(holding up his darts)* I've still got two more darts. Would you like me to…. *(He makes a dart throwing motion)*
TOM	No, Derek, put them away. Other officers will have her by now.

DEREK	*(looking out again)* Oh, yes. That big Bobby just tripped her up. Whoops-a-Daisy!
TYLER	How can Daisy be the inside man, Tom?
TOM	You really didn't know, did you, Tyler?
TYLER	No.
TOM	She's a cleaner there.
TIA	She's not. She's a hairdresser in town.
TOM	Hairdresser by day; cleaner by night. Well, by three evenings a week.
TIA	Really?
TOM	*(nodding and directing Tyler to the door)* Off you go to the waiting officers, Tyler.
TIA	Can I go with him, Tom.
TOM	Sure.

They exit the hall

DEREK	What a day!
MARJORIE	Quite!
DEREK	And we still lost the Games. By one point as well!
TOM	I think you'll find you won, by one point, Derek.
DEREK	How come? We were one point up before I lost the darts, meaning we're now one point down.
TOM	Ah, yes, but Giuseppe was down to play the table tennis and now he can't, it's a walkover for Doris.
DEREK	What?! Yes! You're right! Fantastic! Come on Marjorie, let's tell everyone who's left outside.

MARJORIE *(taking Derek's arm)* Yes. Oh, Doris will be pleased. Getting the winning points aged 87.

DEREK *(leading Marjorie out of the hall)* We won, we won!

Tom sits down in between Sarah and Laura

TOM Well; there we go.

LAURA Yes. All gone.

TOM Sorry, love?

LAURA Giuseppe, Tyler and Daisy. All gone. So the play's gone.

TOM *(smiling weakly)* Sorry, love. I couldn't let it reach the performance dates. Just in case they somehow got away with it.

LAURA I know. I can see that. You could have told me though, couldn't you?

TOM Not really, love. It had to be all hush, hush. Sorry.

LAURA I understand. It's ok.

SARAH Come on, Laura. The show must go on, and all that. Let's recast and set a date later in the year.

TOM Yes; that's it.

LAURA Oh, I don't know.

SARAH The play's too good to just let go, Laura.

LAURA But, recasting the lead roles again. I don't know.

TOM I could do it!

They all smile

LAURA Tom. Bless you.

TOM	Unless I'm too old?
LAURA	*(stroking his face)* Never, Tom.

There's a pause as Sarah looks a little uncomfortable

SARAH	Can I just ask; could you have arrested Giuseppe any time today?
TOM	What do you mean?
SARAH	I mean, could you have arrested him before the darts or after the table tennis?
TOM	I don't know what you're implying?
SARAH	That you gave Derek a chance of glory by letting him play his darts; but when he lost you made sure Giuseppe was unable to participate in the table tennis. Right?
TOM	*(tapping his nose and smiling)* Needs must, Sarah, needs must!
LAURA	*(holding Tom's hand and smiling)* You're a good man, Tom. Do you know that?
TOM	*(eyes fixed on Laura)* Thank you, darling.
SARAH	*(rises and briefly places her hand on Tom's shoulder. He doesn't turn)* Yes. You are a good man. *(She slowly walks towards the exit. Tom and Laura are still sharing a moment. She stops and turns halfway towards the exit)* A very good man. *(She continues, then stops and turns one more time)* Huh. There it is. Real love. *(She exits)*

As Sarah exits lights fade to blackout

The End

FURNITURE AND PROPERTY LIST

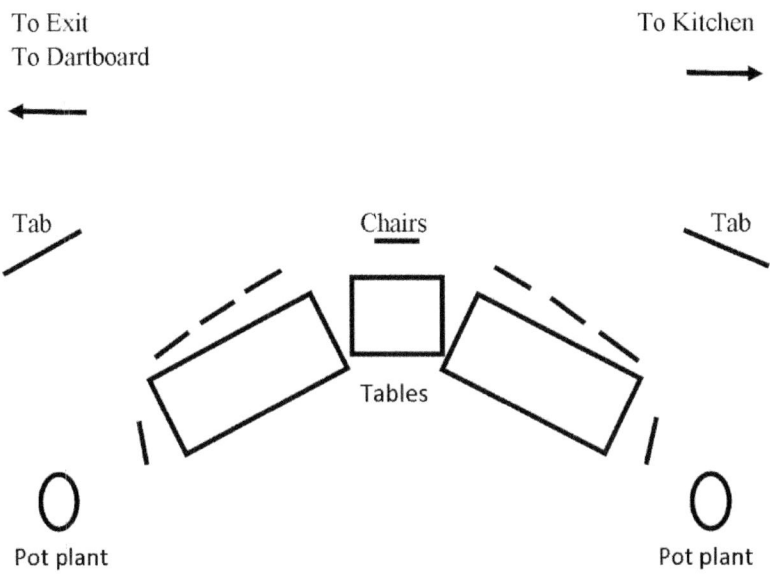

ACT 1

Scene 1

On stage: Tables. *On them:* Pile of plain A4 paper and 6 pencils, sharpened at each end
9 chairs
2 pot plants

Off stage: Plate of biscuits

Personal: **Derek:** Appropriately worded tracksuit top, clipboard with agenda attached
Marjorie: Notepad and pen

Scene 2

Strike:	Biscuits from plate
Set:	6 mugs on table
Personal:	**Laura:** Portable CD player, bag with 8 scripts in

Scene 3

Strike:	6 mugs (plate to be taken off by **Sarah** when she exits to the kitchen)
Personal:	**Tyler:** Key (bent) **Giuseppe:** 2 large plans on scrolls of paper, car keys

ACT 2

Scene 1

On stage:	Exactly the same as ACT 1, Scene 1
Personal:	**Derek:** Clipboard with agenda attached, black marker pen

Scene 2

Strike:	Paper and pencils from table
Personal:	**Tom:** Small electronic device and small screwdriver

Scene 3

Set:	Paper and blunt pencils on table
Off stage:	Tray of mugs
Personal:	**Derek:** Pencil sharpener **Tyler:** Mobile phone

Scene 4

Personal: **Laura:** Portable CD player, bag with 8 scripts in

Scene 5

Set: Tables repositioned nearer kitchen
Mugs and plates on tables

Off stage: Dartboard on stand
Oche mat (rolled on stage by **Tom**)
Darts (**Derek**)

Personal: **Laura:** Portable CD player, bag with 8 scripts in and loose CD
Giuseppe: Darts
Tom: Small remote control

Lighting Plot

- Act 1 Scene 1

Curtains Lights up (Page 1)

At end of Scene: Cue **Marjorie:** Never mind. Shall we make a start? *Fade to blackout* (Page 12)

- Act 1 Scene 2

Lights up (Page 13)

At end of Scene: Cue **Laura:** Books and papers are strewn across her desk.... *Fade to blackout* (Page 26)

- Act 1 Scene 3

Lights up (Page 27)

At end of Scene: Cue **Sarah:** You know that kitchen, Tom. You can hear everything from in there! *Fade to blackout. Curtains* (Page 38)

- Act 2 Scene 1

Curtains Lights up (Page 39)

At end of Scene: Cue **Marjorie:** Although I do think I'll allow myself to open the emergency rations biscuit tin tonight. *Fade to blackout* (Page 48)

- Act 2 Scene 2

Lights up (Page 49)

At end of Scene: Cue **Tom:** Now, then, Marjorie. Let's see if you can get past this! *Fade to blackout* (Page 54)

- Act 2 Scene 3

Lights up (Page 55)

At end of Scene: Cue **Derek:** Now then, the football tournament will kick off first as there're quite a few games to fit in.... *Fade to blackout* (Page 62)

- Act 2 Scene 4

Lights up (Page 63)

At end of Scene: Cue **Laura:** Lovely. Now I'd like to try the scene when Carl's grandmother, Marjorie, meets Bella's mother and father for the first time.... *Fade to blackout* (Page 71)

- Act 2 Scene 5

Lights up (Page 72)

At end of Scene: Cue **Sarah:** Huh. There it is. Real love. *Fade to blackout. Curtains* (Page 90)

Effects Plot

- Act 1 Scene 2 (Page 16)

Cue: **Laura:** Thank you, Tyler. It's my time now. Drama time! *Laura presses play on CD player.* Play 'There's No Business, Like Show Business.' Cut *when Laura presses button again.*

- Act 2 Scene 4 (Page 68)

Cue: **Laura:** Right then. Positions and I'll press play! *Laura presses play on CD player.* Play 'Now or Never (If the Game is to be Won.)' Cut *when Laura presses button again* (page 70).

- Act 2 Scene 5 (Page 79/80)

Cue: **Laura:** As much passion as we can muster this time, please both of you. *Laura presses play on the CD player.* Play 'Now or Never (If the Game is to be Won.)' Cut *when Laura presses button again (not stated) cue:* **Tom:** Game, Derek (page 82).

- Act 2 Scene 5 (Page 84/85)

Cue: **Tom:** I've just been given the signal from outside to play you this. *Points small remote control into the air.* Play *Sarah: 'Ello, 'ello, 'ello, what's going on 'ere then?*
Pause. *Restart cue:* **Tom:** Hang on, wrong bit. Play *Tom: Poof! Sarah: Derek. Poof!*
Pause. *Restart cue:* **Tom:** Erm, sorry, Derek. Technical issues. Try this. Play *Sarah: Put the handcuffs on. Tom: I'll get my truncheon out.* Cut.

- Act 2 Scene 5 (Page 86)

Cue: **Marjorie:** Certainly, dear. *Tom holds up his remote and presses it again.* Play *Giuseppe: We'll be breaking in the day after a big cash delivery, so our insider says. Tyler: Do you reckon six nights under that stage will be enough to get through? Giuseppe: Easily.* Cut.

Printed in Great Britain
by Amazon